GARUDA PURANA

and Other Hindu Ideas on
Death, Rebirth and Immortality

Devdutt Pattanaik has been writing on mythology and its relevance in modern times for the past twenty-five years. Based in Mumbai, in India, he was trained in medicine and worked in the pharma industry for fifteen years before turning his passion into his vocation. He illustrates most of his books, and is also well known for his lectures and TV shows like *Devlok* and *Business Sutra*. His other books by Westland are *Seven Secrets of Hindu Calendar Art, Seven Secrets of Shiva, Seven Secrets of Vishnu* and *Seven Secrets of the Goddess*.

DEVDUTT PATTANAIK

GARUDA PURANA

and Other Hindu Ideas on Death, Rebirth and Immortality

Illustrations by the author

First published by Westland Books, a division of
Nasadiya Technologies Private Limited, in 2022

No. 269/2B, First Floor, 'Irai Arul', Vimalraj Street, Nethaji Nagar,
Allappakkam Main Road, Maduravoyal, Chennai 600095

Westland and the Westland logo are the trademarks of
Nasadiya Technologies Private Limited, or its affiliates.

ISBN: 9789395073448

10 9 8 7 6 5 4 3 2 1

Author's photograph by Harpreet Chhachhia

Design and typeset by Special Effects Graphics Design Co., Mumbai
Printed at Manipal Technologies Limited, Manipal

To my parents,
to my grandparents,
to my great-grandparents,
to all my ancestors before,
and to every other ancestor out there.

Contents

Introduction

*In which we learn about the 3,000-year-old
Hindu ritual of feeding the dead*

During the Indian monsoons—between the ten-day festival of Ganesha (Ganesha Utsava), the elephant-headed remover of obstacles, and the nine-night festival of the Mother Goddess Durga (Nava-ratri)—Hindus observe Pitr-paksha, or the fortnight (paksha, in Sanskrit) of the ancestors (pitr). This is a dark fortnight of the lunar month, in the dark half of the year. It is a time to feed the dead. Facing the south, Hindu men across India are seen placing mashed rice balls mixed with black sesame seeds, known as pinda, on blades of grass, near water bodies. They pour water on these pinda in a peculiar way, known as tarpana, over the thumb of the right hand that is stretched outward away from the body. Crows are encouraged to eat this rice. Every shopkeeper knows business will be slow at this time. Indeed, many Hindu families avoid buying cars or houses or even new clothes. No contracts are signed. No weddings conducted. This hesitance is interesting for what it reveals of the ambiguous relationship Hindus have with the dead. The ancestors are venerated and need to be fed, it's true. However, all things associated with death are also deemed inauspicious and impure.

Pinda-daan, the ritual of
feeding the ancestors

1

Of course, not all Hindus follow these practices and customs. Hinduism is diverse, dynamic and complex. But the dominant mainstream Hindu understanding of death comes from the Preta-kalpa of the Garuda Purana, which was composed a thousand years ago, and is still read during funeral ceremonies. The ritual of shradh that involves offering pinda to ancestors can be traced to Grihya-sutra literature, which is over 2,500 years old, indicating a remarkable continuity of tradition. The word 'pitr' used for ancestors can be traced even to the *Rig Veda*, Hinduism's oldest scripture.

While the practice of giving food and gifts to the dead is found in many cultures, Hindu customs are unique as they are based on the metaphysics of rebirth, not an eternal afterlife. Hindus believe nothing is permanent, not even death. The dead eventually return to the land of the living to repay unpaid debts. Life is needed to free oneself from the burden of debts. Feeding the dead is itself an obligation, a repayment of debt. Those alive owe their life and privilege to the dead. The dead depend on the living to facilitate their return to the land of the living and keep the circle of life turning.

Immersing the ashes and bones of the dead in the river, hoping for their rebirth or liberation

This idea of eternal return is embedded in the Hindu mind through ritual and story. In Vedic times, the ritual arena was set aflame after a yagna—as is done in the case of a funeral— and the altar was then reconstituted with fresh bricks. Today, festivals of Ganesha and Durga are celebrated over ten days and nine nights to remind us of ten lunar months and nine solar months of pregnancy. After the festival, clay effigies of the deity are cast into water bodies, like the ashes of the dead. Thus, even the gods are impermanent. They go away this year but will return next year, mimicking the reality of re-death (punar-mrityu) and rebirth (punar-janma) mentioned in the Upanishads.

Visarjan, the immersion of clay images of deities after ceremonial worship

In the temple of Jagannath Puri, in Odisha, the deity is embodied in a brightly painted image of wood, cloth and resin. Every dozen or so years, the deity grows old and needs to shed his old body. In a secret ritual, the 'soul' of the deity is taken out by a blindfolded priest from a secret chamber of the old body and placed in a secret chamber of the new body. The old body is then buried, and the new body is installed in the temple in a grand ceremony, ready to experience the daily, monthly and annual ritual cycles once again.

Another unique feature of death in the Hindu world view is its association with impurity. If the clockwise orientation is done for the gods, the anticlockwise orientation is reserved for ancestors. Those who visit the crematorium are not allowed to enter the house without bathing. Those whose hereditary occupation was to tend to funeral pyres were deemed 'untouchable', an idea that shaped Hinduism's now illegal caste hierarchy. Women fared no better: menstruating women and widows were also seen as touched by death and so isolated.

That said, the inauspicious funeral ground has also been for centuries the arena of potent power, magic and the occult, the place where gods take fearsome forms like Bhairava and Chamunda, and wander in the company of ghosts and dogs. In many local traditions, the ghosts of ancestors (bhuta) are summoned by shaman-like priests, who wear grand colourful attires and go into a trance in public rituals, to advise and bless the living. In Tantric lore, sorcerers can enslave the ghost (vetala) using the flesh, bones and skull of the dead as ingredients in secret rituals (shava sadhana). To prevent this, people were encouraged to let Brahmins perform the Vedic death rituals, destroying the corpse completely, even smashing its burning skull, to enable the dead to make the journey to the land of the dead, where they can be regularly fed until it is time for their rebirth.

Shiva as the fierce Bhairava carrying the corpse of Sati or Vishvaksena (Kankala-murti), the skull of Brahma or Daksha (Kapalika-murti), begging with his dog (Bhikshatana-murti)

Hindus share their ideas of rebirth with the other faiths of Indian origin, such as Buddhism and Jainism. Myths in most other parts of the world are built around a single life followed by an eternal afterlife. Even in India there are communities such as the Lingayats and the neo-Buddhists who do not believe in rebirth. When you believe you live only once, this life and this body become special. Both are commemorated with tombs and tombstones, a practice shunned by orthodox Hindus who want the dead to move on, not stay back.

There is much to learn about Hindu culture by approaching it through its death rituals. Hence this book with its eleven chapters. Why eleven? To remind us of the odd number of priests invited to the feeding of the dead, in contrast to the even number of priests invited when feeding the gods.

This is an exploratory enterprise, not an academic one. There are no 'arguments' here, or detailed references and citations, but there is an extensive bibliography at the end of the book for those who want to know more. I am fully aware that the funeral rituals have multiple sources, numerous regional and local variations, and many interpretations. This book is a simplified and accessible version of the vast array of information out there. The aim is not to find *the* truth but to appreciate the myriad expressions of Hinduism and expand our mind with new ideas. As in all my books, read on, keeping in mind:

Within infinite myths lies an eternal truth
Who sees it all?
Varuna has but a thousand eyes
Indra, a hundred
You and I, only two.

Devdutt Pattanaik

Chapter 1

Journey of the Dead

In which we learn how the preta makes its journey to the land of the dead, and then returns to the land of the living via the womb

When death occurs in a Hindu household, Brahmins narrate the Preta-kalpa, or Preta-khanda, of the Garuda Purana that describes the journey of the preta, or spirit, after it leaves the corpse, that justifies the need for complex Vedic rituals. Before we familiarise ourselves with that journey, we must appreciate the adventures of Garuda, the celestial eagle, that made him worthy of bringing this knowledge about the afterlife to the human world.

Adventures of Garuda

In the Vedic Age that thrived 3,000 years ago in the Gangetic plains, Garuda was known as Suparna, and he represented the mantras that rose like a falcon and secured for humans the grace of the gods from the heavens. By the Puranic Age, some 1,500 years ago, Garuda had become a mighty eagle, the son of Rishi Kashyapa and his wife, Vinata. The king of all birds and the vahana (mount) of Vishnu, who protects and balances the world, Garuda was the dreaded enemy of the Nagas (serpent beings), a motif that had spread even to Southeast Asia.

In the Puranas, Brahma is called the Creator of the world and the grandfather (pita-maha) of all organisms (jiva). This is because from

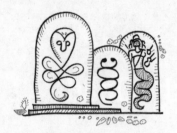

Nagas, the serpent gods

his mind was born Kashyapa, whose many wives gave birth to the diverse living creatures that populate the earth. Through the sisters Kadru and Vinata, Kashyapa became the father of snakes and birds. Kadru and Vinata were rivals. Kadru asked for as many children as could cover the earth and the sky. Vinata asked for just two but wished that their radiance would illuminate the earth, the sky, and the atmosphere in between. Kadru laid millions of eggs and became the mother of Nagas. Vinata laid just two eggs.

Fearing that Vinata's children would enslave hers, Kadru instigated her sister to crack open one of her two eggs and check on the embryo inside. A malformed child emerged, who slipped away and manifested as the mottled sky at twilight. This child had no clear genitals, and so dawn is identified both as the male Aruna and the female Usha. It was clear the eggs contained radiant sun-like children. The next one would be more powerful.

A nervous Kadru tricked Vinata. She challenged her sister to identify the colour of the Ucchaishrava's tail. Ucchaishrava was a celestial horse that rode past the horizon every day. Vinata said it was white. Kadru insisted it was black and wagered her freedom to prove it. Vinata accepted the wager but lost. Kadru used deceit and got her children, the serpents, to cling to Ucchaishrava's tail, making it look black from a distance. Vinata became Kadru's slave. Her child Garuda was thus born into slavery.

The price of freedom was Amrita, the nectar of immortality, jealously

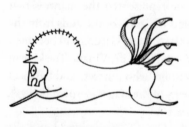

Nagas clinging to the tail of Ucchaishrava, the flying horse

guarded by the radiant Devas, who lived in Swarga, the paradise beyond the celestial regions. Indra, king of the Devas, refused to share his treasure with anyone, especially his half-brothers, the Asuras. You could get something from Indra, only by giving him something, like a hymn of praise accompanying Soma juice

Devdutt Pattanaik

offered during the Vedic ritual of yagna. Garuda used his mighty wings to break into Swarga. There, with his sharp talons and pointed beak, he overpowered the Devas and secured the pot of Amrita. He could have sipped the nectar himself, but Garuda had no desire for what did not belong to him. This earned him the respect of the gods as well as punya, or positive karma.

Garuda gave the pot of Amrita to the Nagas and secured his mother's release. He advised the Nagas to bathe in the Ganga before drinking the nectar. While they were away, the Devas took the pot back to Swarga. Garuda did not stop them, for he was no longer a slave of the Nagas. The Nagas had used trickery to enslave Vinata, and so could not complain against Garuda's trickery. The Devas, grateful to get Amrita back, offered Garuda a boon. He asked that he be allowed to kill the Nagas without earning demerit. That is only possible, said the Devas, if snakes become his natural food. Violence to obtain food and satisfy hunger does not generate negative karma, or paap. This is how snakes became the natural food of eagles.

Garuda feeding on Nagas

In fear, the snakes withdrew to Patala, a realm beneath the earth's surface and devoid of sunshine. They illuminated this domain with the Naga-mani, gems that sprout on the hoods of very old serpents. The older a serpent was the more hoods it would sprout, and each hood could sprout a jewel with time. This jewel contained the power of regeneration known as Sanjivani. This power had seeped into the kusha grass on which the pot of Amrita had been placed. This is why grass regrows when blades are plucked. This is why kusha grass is integral to Vedic rituals. Snakes that slithered on this grass also got the power to regenerate themselves— they could shed their old skin and replace it with a fresh, youthful one.

Garuda's father, Kashyapa, told his son to eat a giant turtle and an elephant fighting each other. Garuda was also asked to hold the branch of a tree to prevent the fall of the thumb-sized Valakhilya sages who were hanging upside down that branch. Garuda wondered about the purpose of these adventures. Go ask Vishnu, said Kashyapa.

Garuda with the elephant, the turtle and the Valakhilyas

Vishnu was the younger brother of Indra, king of the Devas. Unlike Indra, he did not crave the pleasures of Swarga. He reclined on the ocean of milk on the coils of a thousand-hooded Naga called Adi Ananta Sesha. Adi Ananta Sesha means 'primal, infinite residue', referring to the time that exists before, everywhere and after. This Naga was old, as indicated by his infinite hoods and the gems sprouting from each one of them. Unlike other Nagas, Adi Ananta Sesha had condemned his mother's rivalry with her sister. This had earned him the love of Vishnu, who had also condemned the rivalry between the Devas and the Asuras. Devas and Asuras were also children of Kashyapa. Their mothers, Aditi and Diti, were sisters, like Kadru and Vinata.

Vishnu offered to answer Garuda's questions, if the latter agreed to give up anger against the Nagas and serve as Vishnu's mount and take him around the world. Thirsty for knowledge, Garuda agreed to the exchange. That is why the highest wisdom was revealed to him.

Garuda learnt how a half of time is created when the day eats the night and the night eats the day, the eagle eats the snake and the snake eats the eagle, when summer eats winter and winter eats summer. The eaters are eventually eaten. That which feeds will eventually become food. Predator eventually becomes prey and prey eventually becomes predator. Both predator and prey are necessary for life. Devas lose Swarga to the Asuras, but eventually regain it. All victories are impermanent, all defeats temporary. Everyone seeks Amrita, or eternal life. Everyone gets Sanjivani, a chance to regenerate.

Garuda adoring Vishnu seated on the cosmic serpent, Adi Ananta Sesha

Vishnu revealed to Garuda a world full of quarrelling siblings, all grandchildren of Brahma and sons of Kashyapa: Devas and Asuras, Garuda and Nagas, the elephant and the turtle. Ideally, the elephant and the turtle are to serve as foundations of the earth. But by quarrelling, they were creating instability and restlessness. This is how people waste their lives. Being territorial, establishing

Turtle and elephants forming the foundation of earth

pecking orders. One fights for success, to get what is desired. The other fights for justice, to get what is denied. Both feel entitled and assume nature belongs to either, when it belongs to neither. All living creatures, humans included, are just food, to be consumed by the hungry.

But there is a way out from such an existence. This is what the thumb-sized Valakhilya sages communicate as they hang upside down like bats, like caterpillars within pupae before they turn into butterflies.

Long ago, Indra had mocked the tiny Valakhilyas, for even together they could barely carry a twig. The sages said that Indra would meet his match in an eagle called Garuda. Although Garuda would be stronger than Indra, he would also be wiser. He would overpower Indra but not aspire to replace him. He would have the pot of Amrita in his grasp but would not drink it. He would seek wisdom, not wealth or power. That quest for knowledge had brought Garuda to Vishnu.

Vishnu revealed that the dead end up hanging upside down over a bottomless abyss, yearning for another chance to live so that they can utilise the human life to do yoga, and break free of the cycle of rebirth. But once they obtain that human life, that noble goal is forgotten. They are enchanted by the senses (indriya) and their mind (manas) trapped by delusions (maya). Driven by ambition and

Vishnu on Garuda

justice, they become fighting siblings, thus trapped in the ever-turning wheel of life and death (samsara). Having wasted life, by behaving like the foolish elephant and turtle, they return to hanging upside down in death.

How did Vishnu know all this? Because he has witnessed infinite creations and infinite destructions of infinite worlds filled with infinite life forms. Vishnu is the Purusha, described in the Vedas, whose endless limbs and limitless eyes are located everywhere in the cosmos.

Garuda passed on all his learnings to his father Kashyapa, who in turn passed it on to Bhrigu, the sage who travelled the three worlds, from whom it passed to Vasishtha, the guru of the solar dynasty, who told it to Parashara, guru of the lunar dynasty, who passed it on to Vyasa, the organiser of Vedic hymns, who imparted it on the storyteller Romaharshana, who narrated it to the sages in the Naimisha forest, where this knowledge came to be known as the Garuda Purana.

Atma, Dehi, Preta, Pitr

Known as 'Purusha' in the Vedic Samhita, 'Prajapati' in the Brahmana literature and 'Atma' in the Upanishads, the immortal soul is the central character in the story of death. Hindus divide the world into two parts: the mortal half that we experience and the immortal half that we infer. Do we return to this life again, like regenerating plants, reborn from their own seed? Do we stay back in an eternal afterlife? We will never know. Just as the assumption of infinity (ananta) helps humans solve mathematical problems, faith in an immortal soul helps humans live a better, more fulfilled life, facing death fearlessly.

The immortal soul, atma, is wrapped in mortal flesh, or deha. This makes the soul a resident of the flesh, or dehi. Death is called 'dehant', as it is the end (ant) of flesh (deha), not the soul. The atma outlives death. At the time of birth, the atma wears a new body as if it were new clothes, and at the time of death, it discards the old body like old clothes. So says the Bhagavad Gita.

While experiencing life, the flesh experiences various emotions and attachments, such as hunger and fear, jealousy and anger, frustration and vengeance. Unlike animals that forget hunger when their bellies

Devdutt Pattanaik

are full, humans do not forget. Leech-like, they cling to memories and trauma. This eclipses the atma, much like the dust that covers a crystal. Knowledge of the tranquillity (ananda) of the immortal (sada) consciousness (chitta) is obscured by arguments of ambition and aspiration and cravings for justice and fairness. Ambition is about having more than what our siblings have. Fairness is about having at least what our siblings have. We see ourselves alone, separate from those around us. The other is opportunity or threat. The self wants to overpower threats and consume opportunity. The self wants to live at the cost of the other. The finite wants to master the infinite. The limited wants to control the limitless. The mortal wants to direct the immortal. This separation, this fracture, this disunion of jiva-atma and param-atma is what turns the dehi into preta, or the ghost. Trapped in this world, unable to be reborn, the preta become a ghost (bhuta). But it can go to the land of Yama, and live as an ancestor (pitr) and await rebirth, provided living relatives perform the proper death rituals, prescribed in the Garuda Purana.

The Garuda Purana reached its final form probably around tenth century CE. It contains layers of earlier ideas. New editions contain many later ideas too. The rituals can be traced to Grihya-sutras of fifth century BCE. The concepts of liberation can be traced to the Upanishads also of the fifth century BCE. Earlier texts such as Brahmana, and *Srauta-sutra* refer to pinda offerings to pitr. References to a gloomy hell, a radiant paradise, to paths that take us to the land of the gods and the land of the dead are scattered across Vedic literature. The description of the hells is found in the Manusmriti, and many Puranas, such as the Markandeya Purana and the Vamana Purana, dated to fifth century CE. The fearsome imagery of the journey of the dead maps well with Tantric and folklore from the eight century onwards. It resonates with the fourteenth-century *Tibetan Book of the Dead (Bardo Thodol)*, containing the visions of the Vajrayana master, Padmasambhava, that describes the state between death and rebirth as the stepping stones on a river between two shores, a metaphor shared with Vedic literature.

The Garuda Purana is Vaishnav, but in Shaiva traditions these ideas were also shared by Bhairava with the curious Goddess Chamunda. In Bhagavata lore, we learn how Vishnu in the form of Krishna travelled to the kingdom of the dead, ruled by Yama, known as Yama-loka, and brought back the spirit of his guru's son and the spirits of his elder

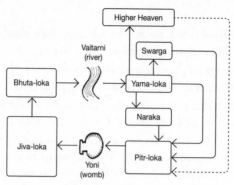

Journey of the dead, as per Hindu mythology

brothers for the momentary pleasure of parents who missed their dead children. The narration of Vishnu to Garuda remains the most popular amongst textual traditions.

The narration of the preta's journey that follows is primarily, but not entirely, based on the Garuda Purana. When reading it, please keep in mind that spiritual ideas are gender-neutral but, to communicate them, traditional writings have used gendered language, symbols and metaphors of the material reality. So, the preta and pitr are identified as male, and ancestors are referred to as 'forefathers' while grandparents are 'grandfathers'. We have tried using gender-neutral language as far as possible.

The journey involves four phases and four destinations. The four phases are: out of the body, wandering around the body, year-long journey to Yama-loka, and finally, Yama-loka itself, also known as Pitr-loka. The four destinations are: the hells (Naraka), paradise (Swarga), higher heavens and eventually, rebirth out of Pitr-loka into the womb (yoni).

Phase 1: Out of Body

Even the old, the sick and the disabled, though unable to eat or digest, move or speak, will still fight for life as they lie dying. Most defy the approach of Yama's emissaries, the dreaded Yama-duta, who appear before them as ugly, gloomy and naked, red eyes and sharp nails, with grinding teeth, bearing noose and rods.

Devdutt Pattanaik

The old human's eyes would have weakened, their throat would be full of phlegm, making sounds like death's rattle drum. They would be unable to communicate with the relatives who surround them. As the senses decay and the mind numbs, Yama's emissaries yank the preta out of their body. Feeling the sting of a hundred

Preta being pulled out of the head of the corpse by Yama-duta

scorpions, mouth full of saliva, throat full of foam, their heart races and they shed excrement as the preta leaves their body. The preta, which is the size of their thumb, looks longingly at the flesh left behind as it is dragged away.

Preta leaves the lifeless body more easily when the body is offered to agni during cremation (mukha-agni), and appropriate Vedic hymns (antyeshti) coax Agni to gently burns the flesh, and the burning skull is cracked open with a stick at the brahmarandra, the top of the cranium.

Phase 2: Wandering around the Body

The preta is lost without its residence. So, after leaving the body, it lingers around the corpse, and in the crematorium, after the body is gone. The Yama-duta catch it like a beast and beat it if it resists capture, as hunters do.

The reluctant preta is yanked towards Yama's abode like a convict, dragged if it does not walk, goaded and pushed, tormented with descriptions of the many hells where it may be tortured. Thirsty and hungry, it walks the path to death's domain, burning in the light, tormented by the sun, by forest fires and hot winds, deprived of shelter and water, whipped relentlessly by fierce winds on a burning path, towards the dark and gloomy realm of Yama.

Banyan trees and pebbles of the crematorium are haunts of the new preta

A lamp is lit at the time of death, giving hope to the lost preta that it has not been forgotten. The temporary body created by the nava-shradh in the ten days after cremation enables it to eat the offerings on its year-long journey that is to follow.

It is memories (smara) and yearnings (kama) that cause these miseries. Birds and animals face no such trauma as they have no memories nor desires. The wise who have let go of memories do not suffer either.

Those that escape the clutches of Yama-duta remain trapped in the crematorium, like ghosts (bhuta) hanging upside down in the likeness of the aerial roots of the banyan tree, a favourite haunt of ghosts. Older abandoned ghosts turn into pishachas who torment more recent pretas. Unlucky ones are captured by sorcerers and turned into slaves (vetala).

The fresh preta has a subtle (ativahika) body made of space, air and heat but it needs a temporary body that can receive food during its long journey to Yama-loka. The ten-part ritual of nava-shradh, mimicking the ten lunar months of pregnancy, is designed to give the new preta that temporary body.

Phase 3: Year-long journey

The lucky ones walk the path of the gods. Most walk the path to the land of the dead, which is a miserable stretch: no shade of trees, no fruit-bearing plants, multiple burning suns, gusts of cold winds that strike like iron whips, a road full of thorns, stinging scorpions, fire, rabid tigers and dogs, hungry owls that peck, mosquitoes that bite, bogs full of leeches, dark wells, hot sands, mounds of ember, showers of blood, weapons, thunderbolts, lakes of pus and blood and excrement that are infested with crocodiles, mists of smoke and flames, vultures circling in the sky, and pits of venomous snakes and rodents.

Torments on the path to the land of the dead

On this path, the wicked who never valued dharma are dragged and pulled by their nose or ear or back with ropes, chains and hooks while being pecked by crows, beaten by Yama's messengers and vomiting blood that they are forced to drink. They walk, mourning and howling at having squandered human life by ignoring dharma.

Some of these bad actions include: not being generous, not making gifts, not worshipping gods, not respecting sages, not making pilgrimages, not helping people, not creating opportunities for others, not digging wells and tanks, not sharing food or donating cows, not respecting lessons from the Vedas, Shastras and Puranas, not respecting elders, not being faithful to one's spouse, not fasting and practising restraint.

In its long journey, the preta reaches many cities, each of which engulfs it with memories and missed opportunities. It regrets loss of family, friends, estates and titles. At every place, it can rest, eat the rice and water provided by living relatives. Yama's minions torment it for wasting its human life and mock it if the preta's relatives have not provided for its food and travel.

Station	City	Timing
1	Saumya	After the first fortnight
2	Sauripura	First month
3	Nagendrabhavana	Second month
4	Gandharvapura	Third month
5	Sailagrama	Fourth month
6	Krauncha	Fifth month
7	Krurapura	Five-and-a-half months
8	Chitrabhavan	The sixth month, where Vaitarni flows
9	Bhawapada	Seventh month
10	Dukhada	Eighth month
11	Nanakranda	Ninth month
12	Sutaptabhavana	Tenth month
13	Rudrapura	Eleventh month
14	Payovarsana	Eleven-and-a-half months
15	Sitadhya	The twelfth month
16	Bahubhiti	The final station before Yama's abode

Across the Vaitarni, either dragged by a hook, or holding the tail of a cow, or in a boat for the lucky ones whose relatives give gifts to the Brahmins representing the ancestors

In the sixth month, the preta must cross the dreaded river Vaitarni, which separates the land of the dead from the land of the living. The river is wide, with piles of skulls and bones and rotting flesh on either bank, its waters full of blood and pus. If the preta has given a gift of a cow in its life, it is entitled to a boat across the waters. If it has not, Yama's minions, who fly above the river, will drag him through the waters by piercing its lip with a hook.

Over the course of a year, having received sixteen offerings at sixteen stations, the spirit finally reaches the city of Yama. These sixteen offerings of the ekodisthta shradh are either offered in sixteen ceremonies through the year, or on the eleventh day after the funeral, for the sake of convenience.

On the twelfth day after the funeral, the sapinda-karana ritual transforms the preta into pitr, and the journey is complete. In this ritual, three names are invoked: the parent who died before, the grandparent before that, the great-grandparent before that too. Here, the preta takes the position of the first pitr, the first pitr becomes the second pitr, the second pitr becomes the third pitr, the third pitr becomes one of the all-gods (vishwadeva)—its name forgotten, and its memory lost to enable its release.

Sapinda (common, or shared, pinda) refers to common ancestors. Siblings and cousins are referred to as 'sapinda' because they share ancestors in common with one. Marriage among sapinda is forbidden in many communities and considered by them to be incest, a behaviour acceptable in animals but best avoided by humans. Hindus differentiate between humans and animals through various rites of passage that constitute the samskara. Samsara is natural; samskara is cultural. In

Devdutt Pattanaik

samsara, there is no funeral or marriage, no clothing or trade, only eating, reproducing and dying. In samskara, there is funeral, marriage, education, clothing and trade.

Phase 4: Yama-loka

As per Vastu-shastra, there are ten directions: above, below, four cardinal and four ordinal directions. Indra is on the east, Kubera on the north, Varuna on the west. The south-west direction is the residence of Goddess Niritti, sometimes merged with Goddess Chamunda, and associated with Mrityu, goddess of death, who separates the flesh and the spirit. The south-east is the abode of Agni, the fire, that consumes the flesh eventually and lights the path towards the land of the dead. And so, it is fitting that Yama-loka is in the south.

The scribe Chitragupta receives his information on the deeds and misdeeds, merits and demerits of all beings from Shravana and Shravani, the ones who hear everything and know the deeds of everyone everywhere and at all times. The house of Chitragupta is surrounded by the quarters of various diseases, from fever to dysentery and rheumatism to pox.

In front of his house is that of Yama himself, who has all the appearance markers of a great king, seated under an umbrella on a bejewelled throne. Around him are the sages and the greatest of kings. His house is full of music and banners. And he holds in his hand a conch shell, a discus, a mace and a sword. His face radiates joy and bliss. This is his good form, meant for those who follow dharma. For the wicked ones who deviate from the path of dharma, Yama manifests his terrible form: on a buffalo, giant and gloomy, rod in hand, unsmiling.

Four roads lead to Yama's house. Those destined for hell for living a life at the cost of

Vayu, the wind that enlivens flesh	Kubera, the lord of treasure	Ishan, the god of regeneration
Varuna, the lord of the sea	Vishnu, who balances all forces	Indra, the lord of the rain
Niritti, the goddess of degeneration	Yama, the king of the dead	Agni, the fire that eats flesh

Guardians of directions, as per Vastu-shastra

Chitragupta, the scribe, receiving information from Shravana and Shravani

others walk the southern path. Those who have been generous all their lives, offering fuel in winter, water in summer, grain during drought, shelter in the rains, nourishing the hungry and thirsty, go by the eastern path. Those who have been brave, fighting thieves and plunderers, and have died defending the weak, walk on the northern path. Those who have lived a life of restraint, repaying all debts, without being jealous, bitter, angry, hateful or unfaithful, walk on the western path.

Yama's doorkeeper Dharmadhvaja announces the presence of everyone who arrives at his door. Those who have been good and honest enjoy benevolence. The bad and the dishonest suffer malevolence and terrible tortures. Yama does not care if one is rich or poor, strong or weak, or about tribe, caste or lineage—all he cares about is actions. These are actions witnessed by the sun and the moon, the dawn and the

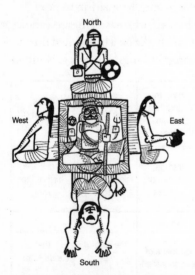

The abode of Yama with four paths for the generous, the brave, the restrained and the rest

dusk, and the five elements, and communicated by the Shravanas and the Shravanis, documented by Chitragupta, and known to Yama.

Yama tells all beings that, after a brief stay in heaven or hell—where they will enjoy or suffer the fruits of their actions, good or bad—they will obtain human life again, and another chance to realise the impermanence of the flesh, wealth, fortune and relationships. Yama advises all to live with restraint and generosity, going beyond the self to help others if they wish to eventually walk the highest path beyond rebirths. Not everyone gets a human life though. Some people

Devdutt Pattanaik

lived lives so filled with bad actions that they are reborn as animals, birds and insects.

Some say that the temporary stay in Swarga, full of pleasures, and Naraka, full of tortures, is a preview of the spirit's future life, of the temporary pleasures and pain he will experience in human life. Others say that those who enjoy Swarga for their merits will be reborn to wipe out whatever demerits they may have accumulated, while those who suffer Naraka for their demerits will be reborn to enjoy whatever little merits they have accumulated. This enables Yama to balance his books. That is why the balance scale is called Dharmakanta, or the needle of dharma—another name for Yama.

The thirteenth-day shradh is a time of festivity, for feeding friends, family and an odd number of Brahmins, to mark the end of the preta's journey to Yama-loka and its transformation into a pitr, ready to receive the offerings made during the parvana-shradh, and await rebirth.

Destination 1: Naraka

Before rebirth, the pitr must experience various hells, each one designed for a crime committed during the last birth. This is the list of hells in the Garuda Purana, grouped by crimes.

Number	Name	Suffering	Crime
1	Tamisram	Flogging	Thieves, including those denying inheritance
2	Rauravam	Snake pit	
3	Maharauravam	Squeezed by a python	
4	Taptamurti	Fire pit	
5	Avici	Hurled from great height	Perjurers, traitors, cheats
5	Sulaprotam	Impaled on tridents	

Number	Name	Suffering	Crime
7	Andhatamisra	Bound and flogged	Committers of sexual crimes, including abandoning spouses, adultery, rape and bestiality
8	Salamali	Red hot metal	
9	Vaitarni	River of blood, pus, excrement	
10	Puyodakam	Pit of sewage	
11	Vajrakantakasali	Embrace pillar of spikes	
12	Lalabhaksham	Semen pool	
13	Ayahpanam	Drink molten lava	Alcoholics who abandon duties
14	Visanam	Beaten and bashed	Show-offs and braggards
15	Ksharakardama	Hung upside down	
16	Sucimukham	Pinned by nails and needles	Stingy and selfish, deniers of food, hospitality, respect
17	Krimibhojana	Eaten by worms	
18	Paryavartanakam	Eyes and flesh pecked by birds	
19	Asitapatra	Whipped with metal blade	
20	Kalasutra	Heat	
21	Sukaramukham	Beaten to pulp	Corrupt, tyrants, oppressors, exploiters, mass murderers
22	Andhakupam	Attacked by animals	
23	Dandasukam	Eaten alive by animals	
24	Sarameyasanam	Ripped by rabid dogs	
25	Kumbhipaka	Boiled in oil	Torturers and killers of animals
26	Pranaraodham	Limbs hacked	
27	Rakshobijaksham	Eaten by animals killed	
28	Vatarodham	Acid and flames	

Devdutt Pattanaik

There are various tortures prescribed: with fire, weapons, acid, animals, serpents, birds, or being beaten, smashed to smithereens, pushed from great heights into pits of sewage and being thrown into rivers of pus. All of these are designed to prevent people from violating their own bodies, and the trust and property of others, and to get householders and kings to do their duties. We find in the ancient texts such as the Mahabharata, Ramayana, Agni Purana and Garuda Purana a great rage against corrupt kings, oppressors, those who torment animals, are proud, stingy, mean, adulterous, abusive, those who brag, insult, rape or commit bestiality, and even those who indulge in oral sex.

Destination 2: Swarga

The Garuda Purana and other Puranas lay a greater emphasis on hells than on heavens. Experience had told the sages that humans respond better to fear than pleasure. Elaborate versions of multiple heavens are found in Jain and Buddhist literature. As in Jainism and Buddhism, the paradise of the gods (Devas) is distinguished as the higher heavens—Vaikuntha, Kailasa, Goloka and Gauriloka—a place for those who have immersed themselves in devotion and outgrown all desires.

Torments of various hells for those with debts to repay

Pleasures of Swarga for those
with good deeds in their credit

Known in Buddhism as the abode of thirty-three gods, Swarga is the eternal abode of the Devas, where good people are welcome and are fed all kinds of food, offered the drink Soma, and invited to witness the dance of apsaras, the song of the Kinnaras and the music of the Gandharvas. This is a place of luxury and indulgence, and of wish-fulfilment. There is the wish-fulfilling tree, Kalpa-taru or Kalpa-vriksha; the wish-fulfilling cow, Kama-dhenu; the wish-fulfilling jewel, Chinta-mani; the vessel Akshaya-patra overflowing with gold and grain; and the garden of eternal delights, Nandan-kanan. Here there is no decay, degeneration or death. Yearnings for such a place are found in the Rig Veda (9.113.7) as the gods are offered the Soma drink, 'Where there is light always, place me in that unperishable, undecaying world.'

Those with meritorious deeds in their credit, those who were generous with gifts and compliments, kind and compassionate, created opportunities for others, were fair and just, performed yagna regularly and fed the gods and the ancestors, and gave back what they received from nature and culture would get to taste the joys of heaven. As long as merits last, one stays in Swarga, and then one tumbles down. Thus, we learn of the kings Yayati and Indradyumna, who were asked to leave paradise after they ran out of merits. Yayati regained heaven when his daughter and grandchildren shared their merits with him. Indradyumna returned when he discovered a turtle who remembered his good deeds. In the Mahabharata, Mahabhisha is also cast out of Indra's heaven because he displays lust at the sight of the beautiful Ganga. He is reborn as Shantanu, whose heart is broken by Ganga.

Those who strive for permanent bliss seek refuge in the higher heavens.

Devdutt Pattanaik

Destination 3: Higher Heavens

In the Mahabharata, there is the story of Rishi Mugdala whom Indra had invited to Swarga. But Mugdala refuses. He says, 'Swarga is for those who have earned merit by performing yagna and feeding the gods, the ancestors as well as those dependent on him, family and friends, servants, teachers, sages, even guests and strangers. But the stay in Swarga is temporary. I want a higher heaven, where the stay is permanent.'

With the rise of the devotional practice of bhakti, and the composition of Puranic literature, this higher heaven becomes specific. The two major heavens are the Kailasa of Shiva and the Vaikuntha of Vishnu. Hermits are welcomed to Mount Kailasa, a place of no hunger—one where Shiva's bull does not seek grass and Shakti's tiger does not hunt the bull. Ganesha's rat is safe from Shiva's serpent, coiled around his neck, and the snake is safe from Kartikeya's peacock. In Vishnu's Vaikuntha, there is plenty for all, as it is located in the ocean of milk (a metaphor for abundance). Unlike Indra's Swarga, constantly under siege by Asuras, there is no battle or conflict in Vaikuntha.

Kailasa, where no one is hungry and the predator and the prey are friends

There are other heavens. There is Brahma-loka for the sages. For the women who have been faithful to their husbands, there is the paradise of Gauri-loka. In Saket, the heaven of Sita and Ram, everyone enjoys the eternal Ram-rajya where dharma is respected by all. In Go-loka, the heaven of Krishna, are the cows that voluntarily give milk and fill the ocean of milk. For those who worship Ganesha, there is Ikshu-vana, or the forest of sugarcane, and for worshippers of Hanuman, there is Kadali-vana, the forest of plantain. From these higher heavens, there is no return to the world of death and suffering. There is only the eternal bliss of enjoying God's face.

However, should the residents show the slightest sign of ego, jealousy, hatred, anger, pride, contempt or attachment, they are cast out, and forced to experience rebirth until it is time again to return to the higher heavens. Thus, we hear of the Yoginis who were cursed and cast out of Kailasa and came to be statues embedded on the throne of King Vikramaditya. They passed on the knowledge of Vikramaditya's kingship to King Bhoja, and were then allowed to return to Kailasa. And in the Bhagavata Purana, we learn of Jaya and Vijaya, the doorkeepers of Vaikuntha, who were cursed by the child-sages, the four Sanat-kumara, for not letting them in. Jaya and Vijaya were reborn as two Asuras (Hiranakashipu and Hiranayaksha), two Rakshasas (Ravana and Kumbhakarna) and two humans (Shishupala and Dantavakra) before they returned to Vaikuntha. So, nothing is essentially permanent, it would appear.

Destination 4: Pitr-loka to Yoni

Pitr hanging upside down above the abyss called Put

The ancestors wait in Pitr-loka patiently until it is time for rebirth. Here, they accept offerings made during shradh. As per the Mahabharata, but not the Garuda Purana, they hang upside down over the bottomless pit called Put, hoping the living will produce children, who will save them from that condition.

Birth is really rebirth. A new life is an old life, carrying the karmic baggage of previous lives, its memories, aspirations and frustrations. After consulting Chitragupta's records, Yama dispassionately determines where one would be born, what would be determined by nature and what by culture. Some believe our gender, sexuality, parents, fortunes are all determined by the karma of the dead (nature). Others believe it is determined by the karma of the living (nurture). Here is a short sample of the list of crimes that, according to the Garuda Purana, impact future lives.

Sample of Crimes	Suffering in Next Life
Killer of Brahmin	Consumptive
Killer of virgin	Leprous
Killer of cow	Imbecile
Killer of woman	Savage
Killer of foetus	Diseased
Sexual deviant	Eunuch
Meat eater	Red-skinned
Alcohol drinker	Discoloured teeth
Greedy	Pot-bellied
Arrogant	Epileptic
Perjurer	Dumb
Book thief	Blind
Liar	Stammerer
Gossipmonger	Deaf
Thief	Poor
Steals food	Rat
Steals grain	Locust
Steals salt	Ant
Hunter	Goat
No offerings to gods	Tiger
Greedy Brahmin	Hog
Unrestrained Brahmin	Crow
Educated who does not teach	Bull
Unruly students	Donkey
Those who torment Brahmins	Fiend
Bad wife	Leech
Oversexed	Horse

Rebirth is only possible when the living relative produces children. That is when pitra-hrinn, or debt to ancestors, is repaid. A man needs a woman and a woman needs a man to repay this debt. A man performing parvana-shradh, and calling three generations of ancestors, assures them that he will enable rebirth by marrying. Those who do not marry, or have no children, have to perform special shradh in pilgrim spots for themselves. There is a way out for all. Ancestors who feel forgotten often trouble the living and so special shradh rituals such as Narayana-bali must be performed to calm them down. In Narayana-bali the angry pitr are elevated to Vaikuntha by the grace of Vishnu. Pleased, they shower blessings on the living.

Vedic texts enumerate rites of passage to enable the birth of children. This includes marriage (vivaha), which is a social event. Then, at the appropriate time, the husband is expected to be intimate with his wife. This is the samskara of conception (garbha-dana). Marriage was separated from conception, for sometimes the bride and groom are not mature enough to be intimate. Sometimes, the husband lacks the capacity to make his wife pregnant. In ancient times, women were allowed to go to other men to make a baby. This practice was called niyoga. For example, in the Mahabharata, King Vichitravirya dies prematurely and Vyasa is sent to his widows, Ambika and Ambalika, so that they can become mothers of the future rulers of Hastinapur.

The Garuda Purana as well as several Tantric texts elaborate the process by which the pitr enters the womb of a woman and gets embodied. Details vary. The penis needs to rise in pleasure and excitement, and enter a consenting, joyful womb, filled with happy vibrations, and leave the white seed within before withdrawing. In art, when the woman is above the man, it indicates her consent.

When the white seed of man joins the red seed of woman, the

bleeding of the womb stops, and a few days later, a new child is conceived. The white seed is ever ready to turn into a new life, but the red seed, like nature, is changing constantly. The window of opportunity is short and difficult to control, and the white seed struggles to succeed. What happens in the womb imitates the stresses outside the womb: the uncontrollable passage of time (kala) and the struggles with rival sperms.

Concentric layers of flesh (kosha) that encircle the soul

From the father, the embryo gets bones

Devdutt Pattanaik

and nerves. From the mother, it gets flesh and blood. When the white seed is strong, a male child is born. When the red seed is strong, a female child is born. When both seeds are of equal strength, the queer child is born. In some, the flesh may be ambiguous. In others, the sexuality will not match the flesh.

Over ten lunar months, the food consumed by the mother transforms into the five elements that develop into multiple layers (kosha): flesh, breath, sensations, emotions and intelligence. Earth gives skin, bones, hair, flesh and nerves. Water gives saliva, urine, sperm, marrow and blood. Fire enables hunger, thirst, desire, sloth and sleep. Wind enables bending, walking, running, jumping and stretching. Ether enables speech, thought, sensations, emotions and delusions.

Multiple tissues (dhatu) develop in the body: lymph, blood, flesh, nerves, bones, marrow and genital fluids. Some sense organs also receive stimulus from the world (gyan-indriya) outside: ear, eyes, nose, skin and tongue. The body's action organs respond to these inputs from the world (karma-indriya): hands, feet, mouth, anus and genitals.

The body which engages with the world around us is our outer reality. Within is the inner reality. Inputs received from the outside world generates sensations in the mind (manas), emotions in the heart (chitta) and thoughts in the head (buddhi) that are judged by the ego (aham), all invisible aspects of the inner reality.

There are multiple levels of awareness locked in the nodes of the spine (chakra): fear of death, craving for pleasure, hunger for food, yearning for love, communication, insight and wisdom. The left side of the body is controlled by the right side of the head, which shines like the sun (pingala), and the right side is controlled by the left side of the head, which waxes and wanes like the moon (ida). Each chakra is connected to every part and pore of the body through channels (nadi)—the central one (shushumna) offering the coiled serpent (kundalini) a chance to rise and awaken the bud in the head to bloom like a thousand-petalled lotus.

In the womb, the child remembers its past lives, and hopes to make the best of the new

Tantric understanding of the body with chakra and nadi

Man and woman come together to enable rebirth

opportunity of a human life. But the trauma of childbirth causes it to forget. This death of old memories, which would have aided its quest for liberation, is mourned over ten days. That is why, for ten days after the birth of the child, the household is deemed impure, unworthy of touch. This period of purification is called 'sutaka'. It mirrors the period of purification in the ten days after death. At both times—birth and death—the land of the dead and the land of the living come in close contact, first in the womb, then at the birthing couch, and finally at the deathbed and cremation ground.

Devdutt Pattanaik

There are many rituals for the dead in Hinduism. They all presuppose the journey of the dead described in the Garuda Purana. But there is diversity across history, geography and communities.

These rituals can be traced to three thousand years ago. But they have evolved over time. Here is a summary. The Rig Veda provides funeral hymns. The Shrauta-Sutra invites ancestors to meals. The Grihya-sutra elaborates the shradh. The Dharma-shastra turns Brahmins into representatives of the dead. The Ramayana marks the shift from burying ashes and bones to immersing them in a river. The Puranas propagate the idea of pinda-daan at pilgrim spots and Bhakti literature prescribes chanting God's name to liberate the soul.

What follows is an overview of these diverse rituals for the Hindu ancestor. The major rituals include:

1. **Funeral rituals**

    a. **Antyeshti:** cremation and casting the bones and ashes in a river

    b. **Nava-shradh:** the ten-part creation of a temporary body for the preta for ten days after the funeral, often compressed into a single ritual

c. **Ekodishta-shradh:** providing food and other provisions for preta's journey, over one year, now compressed to the eleventh-day ritual. The annual death ceremony is also called ekodistha shradh, as it focuses on a single person.

d. **Sapinda-karana:** the transformation of the preta into a pitr, at the end of the year, now performed on the twelfth day

e. **Shradh-bhog:** the feast to mark the end of mourning and inauspicious period with the transformation of preta into pitr, where an odd number of Brahmins are given gifts and fed

f. **Varshik-shradh:** the annual death anniversary ritual feeding of the dead

2. **Feeding rituals**

   a. **Parvana-shradh:** routine feeding of the collective of ancestors daily, monthly and, most importantly, annually, during Pitr-paksha

   b. **Tirtha-shradh:** feeding of ancestors at a pilgrim spot, to mark the end of death anniversary rituals

   c. **Narayana-bali:** special feeding to appease ancestors who died by violence or accident, and so are angry, dissatisfied, restless and cause misfortunes, as indicated by astrologers (pitru-dosh)

   d. **Vriddhi-shradh:** to celebrate happy occasions with auspicious ancestors (nandimukha-pitr) when the usual inversion of ritual orientation associated with death is not conducted

3. **Chautha:** memorial meeting

When the ritual is described in the manuals, it is assumed that the performer (karta) is the dead person's son. A jivaputrik is one whose father is alive and is performing rituals for someone else, either for his mother or his maternal grandfather, who had no sons. Nowadays rituals are performed by women too. Before the advent of television, funeral rituals were known only to men, as women were not allowed to enter crematoriums or attend feeding ceremonies.

Funeral Ritual	Purpose	Time
Antyeshti (mukha-agni and asthi-visarjan)	Disposal of the body by fire and water	Within twenty-four hours of death
Nava-shradh with ten puraka rituals	Preta with ativahika body given a jatana body	Ten days after the funeral but sometimes done at once either after the funeral or on the eleventh or twelfth day
Ekodishta shradh performed for a year	Providing provisions to enable safe travel to Yama-loka	Over the first year (now done on the eleventh day mostly)
Sapinda karana (the last of sixteen major rituals of ekodishta shradh)	Transforming preta into pitr	First death anniversary but now done on the twelfth day mostly
Parvana shradh	Routine feeding collective ancestors	Monthly or annual feeding ritual

Antyeshti

Antyeshti is also known as 'antim kriya' or 'antim sanskar', the last rite of passage. It involves taking the body to the crematorium, lighting the funeral pyre, breaking the skull, and ends with the collection of ashes and bones to immerse it in a river.

Hindu cremation must take place soon after death, preferably within twenty-four hours, to enable the quick departure of the preta to the Pitr-loka. Many Hindus, especially the 'upper' castes in North India, prefer cremating the dead. The cremation ground is usually located on the southern side of the village, the direction ruled by Yama, and preferably near a water body. Hindus who choose to bury the dead sometimes conduct shradh rituals, nevertheless.

Children, however, are buried under trees in the cremation ground (smashan-bhoomi), or cast into a river, their bodies consumed by earth and water and worms, fish and turtles. When young people die before marriage, rituals for them are different, and simpler, as their preta is treated kindly by Yama-duta.

The corpse is not addressed by name. At home, the body is placed in the north–south axis, with feet pointing south, indicating its movement towards Yama-loka. However, during cremation, the feet point north, so that the preta leaving from the aperture in the skull travels immediately and straight in the southward direction, towards Yama-loka.

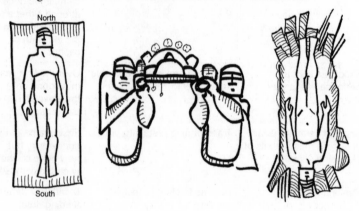

Orientation of the body at home, on way to crematorium, and on the pyre

Some families pour a little Ganga-jal (water of the Ganga) into the mouth of the dead before the body is carried to the cremation ground. The body is typically wrapped in cloth. If the dead is a woman whose husband is still alive, she is bedecked as a bride. The body is anointed with sandal paste to indicate a householder's life, and ash to indicate a hermit's life. Sandal paste is made using water and ash with fire. This water-and-fire connection is a recurring theme in the rituals. Water is feminine, fire is masculine. Water is Ganga, fire is Shiva. Sandal paste is Vishnu, ash is Shiva. Fire and water from the house are taken in pots to the crematorium.

Devdutt Pattanaik

Traditionally, the rituals were performed by men. Now, women also participate. At the cremation ground, the chief mourner goes around the body counterclockwise, carrying a water pot on his left shoulder. The pot is cracked three times so that water pours out in three streams to his back as he walks. After three rounds, the mourner drops the pot behind him. Thus, symbolically, the ghost is told to let go of his three bodies: social, physical and mental.

Fire pot on the way to the crematorium and water pot during the funeral

The body is covered with ghee, that is, clarified butter. Five balls of rice or barley, the pinda, are placed on the head, shoulders and palms, to serve as food for the Yama-duta. Gold is also placed on the body. This was later collected by the Chandala, the traditional keepers of the crematorium, who have a right over everything given to the dead. The karta circles the body in a counterclockwise direction as he sets the pyre alight. This is called the mukha-agni, the giving of fire. If the deceased is male, the fire is lit from the head. In the case of women, it is lit from the feet. To stoke the pyre, straw, coconut husk and cow dung cakes are added to the wood. Hymns from the Rig Veda (10.16.1)are chanted, 'Don't burn him entirely; don't scorch his body; don't singe his skin. When cooked to readiness, impel him forth to the forefathers.'

As the flames consume the body, the chief mourner is asked to take a bamboo pole and smash the skull. This allows the preta to escape the body. Nowadays, in electric crematoriums, this ritual is not possible, so it is symbolically performed by overturning the pot of fire on the chest of the corpse before it is taken into the incinerator. After the rituals, when it is time to leave the cremation ground, no one turns back. It is time to let go. Those who

The breaking of skull at the Brahmarandra spot to help the preta leave the body

visit the cremation ground are asked to bathe before returning home. They also touch a cow, some grain, milk and images of gods to restore their purity.

In the old days, the Chandala kept watch over the funeral pyre, ensuring that the body burnt until it was consumed. He kept dogs and crows from grabbing a charred limb. His income came from the services he provided. He had rights over everything that was given to the dead and survived the flames, including gold and gems.

The next day, milk is poured on the embers. Then the ash and bones are collected in a pot, tied in a cloth and hung from a tree or a hook on the wall, ensuring that it does not touch the ground. At a suitable date in the future, these ashes and bones are cast into a river (asthi-visarjan), where the final shradh ritual is performed.

No one visits the house of the dead. Even the relatives of the dead who do not live in the same house are considered impure until the sapinda-karana ritual is completed on the twelfth day. This period of impurity is called 'sutaka'. Post-cremation rituals used to go on for a year but currently are done within thirteen days, oftentimes in one day.

Nava-shradh

Lamp, water, germinating seeds, and the pot of ash and bones giving hope to preta as a temporary body is being created

Between the cremation and the sapinda-karana ritual, the preta is granted a temporary body to enable it to eat and drink on its journey to the land of the dead. This is the purpose of the nava-shradh, 'nava' meaning new or the first shradh for the recently deceased.

After the preta has escaped the body through the cracked skull, it lingers in the crematorium, either in a nearby pipal tree or a rock (preta-shila). A pot filled with drinking water is tied to a tree branch, with a lamp hanging above it and some seeds scattered at the foot of the tree. The lamp above guides the preta and the seeds below germinate, giving hope of rebirth to the now terrified ghost which has a subtle (ativahika) body made of air (vayu), space (akash) and heat (tejas). The preta can see and hear but cannot eat. For that, a new temporary body (jatana deha) is needed. It is created through puraka over ten days (ten rituals) of the nava-shradh. This body enables the preta to travel to Yama-loka and become a pitr eventually.

In the days that follow, the karta holds one mashed rice ball in the right hand every day, over which he pours water containing black sesame seeds. On the first day, one spoonful of water is poured. On the second day, two spoonfuls. By the tenth day, ten spoonfuls of water are poured on the pinda. Each day, this ritual creates a different part of the body for the preta. With this body, the ghost can travel to the land of ancestors. It will now also be able to experience hunger and thirst, and receive the food offered by relatives. The ten-day ritual is a reminder of the ten lunar months of pregnancy when the ghost gets a new body in a mother's womb. Nowadays, these ten-day rituals are conducted on the day of the funeral itself.

Day	Body Part
1	Head
2	Neck and shoulders
3	Heart and chest
4	Back
5	Stomach and trunk
6	Thighs and bowels
7	Feet and skin
8	Knees and hair
9	Genitals
10	Digestion

Creation of the temporary body

During this period, the Preta-kalpa of the Garuda Purana is read entirely. Translated in local language, it describes the journey of the dead to Yama-loka in gory detail. This journey takes a year, and it involves sixteen resting spots and crossing the river Vaitarni. The journey is terrifying, made worse if the dead are not provided with the comforts of travel, including food, footwear, clothes, bags and mattresses. The mourners are asked to give this to Brahmins, who stand in for the dead. This, the karta is assured, will make the journey to Yama-loka pleasant for their loved ones. The mourners are reminded that the preta could be dragged across the dreaded river Vaitarni by flying Yama-duta who use curved nails to hook them by their lips. This suffering can be prevented by giving the Brahmin a cow, the tail of which the preta can grab to stay afloat and swim across. If gold is given, even a boat can be made available.

Head full of hair (worldly life)

Tuft of hair on the scalp (return to household life)

Shramana monk (shaven head exposed)

Brahmin monk (shaven head, covered)

Yogi (matted hair)

Meaning of hair on the head

Ekodishta-shradh

From the eleventh day onwards, the fully formed preta is offered food and water by the living offspring for its long journey to the land of the dead. The food is mashed rice, for the preta's body has everything but teeth so that it cannot bite anyone.

Traditionally, simple rituals would happen every day of the year until the sapinda-karana ritual, with elaborate rituals on new-moon nights and additional rituals that add up to a total of 360 daily rituals and sixteen monthly rituals. Nowadays this is done on the eleventh day itself using sixteen mashed rice balls and 360 barley cakes. Since this ritual takes place in memory of the deceased, it is called ekodishta-shradh, as opposed to sarva-pitra shradh that is for all ancestors and not any one in particular.

The ritual involves sixteen pindas. The jump from ten pindas of the nava-shradh to sixteen of the ekodishta-shradh also indicates the rising hunger of the preta. The number also refers to the sixteen days of Pitr-paksha, which begins from the full moon in the month of Bhadrapada and ends with the following new moon marked.

The number 'sixteen' harks back to the creation hymn from the *Shatapatha Brahmana*, which tells us that creation involves the Prajapati being split into sixteen

Devdutt Pattanaik

parts: from the golden egg (Hiranya-garbha) emerges two genders, the day and the night, the three worlds, the four directions and the five elements.

During this ritual, the standard ritual orientation is changed. Instead of east, the karta faces south. The sacred thread and upper garment hang on the right shoulder, the left knee rests on the ground, the movements are counterclockwise, the left hand is sometimes used, and water is always poured away from the body over the outstretched right thumb.

Brahmins are meant to represent the dead and are invited in odd numbers. They are given gifts such as clothes, footwear, money, mattresses, bags, utensils and grain. They haggle a lot. This is a ritual to indicate the dissatisfaction of the dead. The Brahmins invited to funeral rituals are differentiated from Brahmins involved in marriage rituals, thread ceremonies and temple worship. These old hierarchies are slowly losing their relevance though.

Sapinda-karana

The sapinda-karana ritual, which transforms the preta into a pitr, was originally performed a year after a person's death—the duration of the preta's journey to the Pitr-loka, that is, Yama-loka. It is the last of the sixteen ekodishta-shradh. This is now done on the twelfth day after the cremation. Thus, rituals adapt to the realities of the day.

Siblings and cousins with common parents, grandparents and great-grandparents are called 'sapinda', for they offer pinda to common ancestors. These are the relatives who are affected by sutaka or impurity during birth or death in family.

The men of the group are encouraged to shave their heads as a mark of mourning when someone dies. Hair has great significance in Hinduism. It is an indicator of fertility and virility. The well-oiled and combed hair indicates domestication and culture. The unkempt hair indicates wild, untamed energy. The matted hair of yogis indicates power over the material world. The fully shaved head indicates complete renunciation and is reserved for monks and widows. As this is considered inauspicious in Hinduism, the shaven head is covered with a cloth. In funeral rituals, when the head is shaved, care is taken that a tuft of hair is left on to remind them they are not hermits but householders. They must return to the world of the living. It has been observed that funerals often cause people to temporarily lose interest in life. This is called 'smashana vairagya', or the detachment that is provoked by witnessing cremations.

For the sapinda-karana, the preta's pinda is made as an oblong rice cake. Three rice balls are also made, representing the preta of the father, grandfather and great-grandfather of the deceased, who live on earth (bhu), the atmosphere (bhuvah) and the sky (svahah). The ancestors before them exist in the transcendent space beyond the sky with the all-gods (vishwadeva). These four rice balls are mixed and mashed together to create three new balls. The son who performs the ritual is either blindfolded or made to look away during this ritual because, as the process of transformation takes place, the dreaded portal between the lands of the living and the dead is open. With this ritual, the preta becomes a first-generation pitr. His father's pitr becomes a second-generation pitr, and his grandfather's pitr a third-generation pitr. And his great-grandfather's pitr goes to the great beyond, to join the vishwadeva. Sometimes four pots of water are kept, three for the old ancestors and one for the recently deceased. The water is mixed to ritually change status of the recently deceased. When the preta becomes a pitr, the journey is complete.

Pitr	Relationship	Location	Status
First	Parent	Earth	Vasu
Second	Grandparent	Atmosphere	Marutta
Third	Great-grandparent	Sky	Aditya
Infinity	Those who came before	Beyond	Vishwadeva

Third pitr (great-grandparent)

Second pitr (grandparent)

First pitr (parent)

Recently deceased, who will join ranks of pitr

The preta-pinda form of recently deceased is mixed with the tri-pinda, triple form of earlier ancestors, to transform preta into pitr

Once this journey is concluded, the ash and bones from the cremation, all the funeral ritual objects, including the pots used to water the preta, the geminated sesame and cooked rice, are immersed in a river, preferably Ganga, or at a pilgrim spot like Pehowa, Gaya, Nashik or Rameshwaram.

Until the karta, the chief performer, can go to a pilgrimage spot and conduct the final shradh, all this material is kept tied above the ground. Until then, each year, on the death anniversary of the deceased, pinda-daan is offered to the dead. Since the ritual focusses on a single dead relative, and not to the ancestral collective, it is called ekodishta-shradh.

Shradh-bhog

On the thirteenth day a huge feast is organised to mark the successful completion of post-cremation ceremonies. The preta has become a pitr and is safe in Yama-loka and will visit the land of the living with other ancestors at ritually scheduled times. Traditional meals served at this ceremony use ancient recipes from before the advent of tomato, potato and chillies. They usually contain yam and pepper. Nowadays, the favourite food of the deceased is cooked so that relatives remember him fondly.

An odd number of Brahmins are invited for the feast. Their satisfaction refers to satisfaction of the ancestors. This practice of using Brahmins as mediators and substitutes for ancestors, and not just as ritual priests, began with the Grihya-sutra and is endorsed by the Dharma-shastra.

Feeding an odd number of Brahmins and giving them gifts that will help the deceased on their journey to Yama-loka

Tirtha-shradh

At one time, the ritual of feeding ancestors (pinda-daan, or pitra-yagna) was part of grand public ceremonies. But they became increasingly private and domestic as society became cosmopolitan. With time, families found it difficult to perform too many shradh rituals. So, to terminate the ritual, Hindus are advised to travel to pilgrim spots such as Gaya, Kurukshetra, Haridwar, Kashi, Nashik, Puri, Srirangam and Rameswaram, take a bath in the waters and then perform shradh there.

In these places, the funeral offerings are given to God, who offers them endlessly to the ancestors. This belief became widespread in the last thousand years, with the popularity of temples and pilgrim routes. We know this because the 2,000-year-old Dharma-shastra does not explicitly refer either to temples or pilgrimages. But these themes become very important in commentaries to the very same Dharma-shastra, which come about a thousand years later. This indicates that the orthodox Vedic Brahmins endorsed temple practices much later.

Feeding crows who represent ancestors

Parvana-shradh

Shradh means feeding the ancestors with reverence (shraddha). Feeding a single ancestor is called ekodishta-shradh, while ceremonial feeding the ancestral collective (sarva-pitr) during special occasions is called parvana-shradh. Some feed the ancestors every day. Some do it every new moon day, or on the ninth day of the waning moon. Most commonly, the feeding takes place on Pitr-paksha, the fortnight of ancestors. Here offerings are made to dead parents, grandparents, great-grandparents, to ancestors who existed before them, as well as to all others who reside in the land of the dead.

The feeding of the ancestors begins first by feeding the gods, then the sages and finally the ancestors. At each stage, the karta takes up different positions and performs different gestures as described below.

The pinda representing the ancestor is placed on kusha grass pointing southwards, representing a sacred mat. The ancestor is offered many things: lamp (dipa), incense (dhup), threads to indicate cloth (vastra), cosmetics (indicated by collyrium, vermillion, turmeric, sandal paste), rice for nourishment, sesame for flavour and ease of digestion, and water for thirst.

In the old days, ancestors were offered not just rice but also other grains, cereals and beans. They were also offered their favourite food: fish as well as meat of wild and domestic birds and animals, including the meat of carp, crane and goat. These practices are mentioned in the Dharma-shastra. But today, these ideas are ignored—even denied by religious leaders who want to promote the belief that Hinduism is essentially vegetarian. In Bhasa's *Pratima Nataka*, a Sanskrit play based on the Ramayana, Ravana disguises himself as a Brahmin and tells Ram that, to feed his dead father, he must offer the meat of the rare golden deer. While Ram is away pursuing that deer, Ravana abducts Sita.

Recipients of food	Gods	Sages	Ancestors
Stance of the feeder	Savya (Yagnopaviti)	Niviti	Apasavya (Prachinaviti)
Sacred thread hangs on	Left shoulder	Around neck	Right shoulder
Upper garment hangs on	Left shoulder	Around neck	Right shoulder
Raised knee	Left	Seated cross-legged	Right
Resting knee	Right	Seated cross-legged	Left
Facing	East	East	South
Water poured on food	Over right palm	Through right fist	Over right thumb
Movements	Clockwise	Clockwise	Anticlockwise
Ritual Exclamation	'Svaha!'	'Svaha!'	'Svadha!'

Narayana-bali

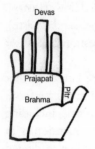

Parts of the right palm mapped to venerable beings

Sometimes, shradh is performed when misfortune strikes the family and astrologers suspect that it is the result of the ancestors being angry. Angry ancestors include those who died in violence or accidents and for whom proper rituals were not performed. Or they can be ancestors whose wishes are not fulfilled and who are unable to move on to the next life.

To appease these angry ancestors the Narayana-bali shradh is performed. Due attention is given to forgotten or overlooked pitr. Done well, it can even elevate the ancestors from Pitr-loka to Vaikuntha, the abode of Vishnu, and so bring fortune back into the lives of the living.

In the Garuda Purana, this ritual was instituted by King Babruvahana. While on a hunting trip, he encountered hungry and angry ghosts in the forests. Feeling sorry for them he decided to perform rituals to feed them even though they were not his own relatives. A good king cares not just for the living but also for the dead, not just for his subjects but also strangers.

The Bhavishya Purana recommends other rites for those who died and whose body could not be found. Effigies are made either using kusha grass or vegetables. They are cremated and shradh rituals are performed. This is done after waiting for twelve years for a person to return. If he does return after his 'funeral rites', he has to undergo 'samskara' rites where he is symbolically reborn and then symbolically remarried.

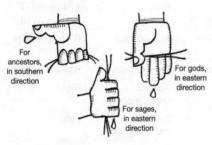

Hand gestures to feed the gods, the sages and the ancestors

Vriddhi-shradh

Some people want ancestors to attend important celebrations in the family, such as marriage and childbirth, and invite them to eat. This is the vriddhi-shradh, nandi-shradh or abhyudaya-shradh, a unique ritual among the various shradh rites, because the ancestors are welcomed as pure beings. That is why an even number

Feeding gods and ancestors on happy occasions

of Brahmins are fed, unlike an odd number of Brahmins in all the other shradhs. Moreover, the rites of inversion seen during the shradh ceremonies are minimised or absent altogether here.

Chautha

Many Christian communities observe the practice of wake, where relatives and friends gather in the house of the dead to remember them and join in to have a meal together. The word 'wake' comes from the practice of staying awake and keeping vigil around the dead before and after burial. This is to ensure that the ghost of the dead does not return to the land of the living. Many Hindu communities have similar practices. Known as Chautha in Hindi-speaking areas and Besnu in Gujarat, this involves gathering to remember the dead, on the third or fourth day after death. Unlike the Christian

Although Vedic rites discourage memory of the dead, modern photography allows us to remember and venerate loved ones.

wake, where people dress in black, Hindus wear white. Prayers and chanting are performed to comfort the living. Flowers are offered to a photograph or image of the dead. Usually, there is no feeding—that is reserved for the shradh on the thirteenth day.

These practices are modern rituals, not referred to in traditional Vedic scriptures. They coincide with the day the bones and ashes are collected in a pot after cremation. In Vedic times, this pot was buried but in post-Vedic times the ash and bones were cast in a river. This is probably when the extended family (not present at the funeral held within a day of the death) gathered to mourn.

Memorial services allow friends and relatives to offer condolences to those immediately affected by the death. Spiritual conversations and chanting of hymns help cope with loss. Sometimes this is when the will is read out by lawyers. If the head of the household dies, this is when the heir is formally announced. The occasion is solemn and contrasted with the thirteenth day ritual when the feast marks the end of the mourning period.

All death-related rituals are as much for the living as for the dead. Rituals help the bereaved cope with loss. In the absence of rituals, there is nothing for the living to do but brood on the horror of mortality and the gut wrenching emotions of loss. This can lead to pathos and depression. Rituals hand-hold those living to mull over loss and life and reshape the new meaning of life that follows.

Chapter 3

Memorials for the Dead

In which we learn about why Hindus avoid building tombs, except viragal, chhatris and samadhis meant for heroes, kings and saints

In the world view of the Garuda Purana, to remember the dead is to prevent them from moving on to the land of the dead and from there to the next destination. The rituals are, in fact, designed to urge the ghost to move away from the land of the living. This is also why only three generations of ancestors are remembered, and the ones before are believed to exist in the great beyond with the nameless all-gods. No likenesses are raised in their honour, no monuments built. The old clothes are discarded so that they can be forgotten by the dead, leaving them free to seek new clothes or freedom from clothes.

But all Hindus do not follow the orthodox Vedic way. Times have changed too, as have social mores even among upper-caste Hindus. Besides, there are burial sites, dolmens, stupas, samadhis, hero stones, cenotaphs and sepulchres aplenty across India to remind the living of the dead. Across India, we find ballads (mahatmya) and genealogies were composed to remember eminent personalities. In Haridwar, there are specialists who maintain records of the family tree of pilgrims who visits these sites. Copper plates and stone inscriptions are kept, maintaining records of rights over land, water and ritual. So, memory of the ancestors has not totally been abandoned.

Burials

In Harappan burial sites, women typically wear bangles in their left arm

Before the rise and spread of Vedic culture, most people in the Indian subcontinent buried their dead. Prehistoric burials had the dead buried either flat on their back, or crouched in foetal position, directly in the ground, or in coffins or pots, with funeral material such as jewellery, mirrors and pots containing food. Sometimes a pair was buried together. The burial spot was marked by a stone. In agricultural communities, these markers helped establish property rights.

In Harappa, bodies were buried in the north–south direction, with the head placed towards the north, the feet facing the south—a practice still followed in India today when the body is kept in the house, before being taken to the crematorium. Women were buried with bangles and a mirror. In Bagpat, Sanauli, Uttar Pradesh, coffins dated to 1800 BCE have been found buried with wagons, probably pulled by oxen. These practices indicate belief in an afterlife, the idea that one goes to another world after death, a plane where the deceased will need the material comforts of this world. These ideas are common beliefs across the world.

Saints are buried in the seated position

Burial was practiced in Aryan communities found in Central Asia and Oxus regions. Historians are of the opinion that Vedic culture emerged when Aryan men married local women who may have introduced cremation. This verse from the Rig Veda (10.18.11) reminds us that burial was practised even in Vedic times. 'Open up and do not crush him, dear earth. Let it be easy for him to enter and burrow in, dear earth. Wrap him as a mother wraps a son in the edge of her robe, dear earth.' But eventually cremation became the high tradition, for it offered the chance of rebirth.

Devdutt Pattanaik

Many communities in India continue to bury the dead on The bodies are often placed in a seated position, especially for elders. The body is covered with salt to prevent noxious odours of rotting flesh from rising. Food, clothes and water is often placed next to them.

Pot Burials

There are very few burial sites in Harappa when compared to the vastness of the civilisation's population. It is believed that many probably cremated the dead, threw the bodies in rivers or exposed them to the elements. The practice of collecting bones after cremation and putting them in pots too has been noted in Harappa. Funeral pots from the period show images of peacocks, and it is possible that they may have believed that these birds enabled the journey to the afterlife. We find extensive use of pottery in burial, a practice that continues even today.

Harappan funerary pot with bones inside and peacock motif outside

In the Iron Age, burial inside pots was common among tribal communities across India. Pot burials dating to 1000 BCE have been found in Daimabad and are now being discovered in many parts of Tamil Nadu. The body was put in a large earthen pot, in a foetal or seated position, given some rice and cloth, covered with salt and turmeric, and the pot was then put in a pit and covered with a large stone, with a menhir-shaped rock (also referred to as 'pinda') marking the burial spot.

Tamil Sangam poetry, dated to 100 CE, captures the memory of a pot burial. It also speaks of wives accompanying their husbands in death. 'Maker of the burial pot, like the small white lizard which clings to the cart and travels long distances, I have travelled with this man, so make the pot big for the both of us.'

Symbolic Burials

Although Harappan cities appear to have been remarkably organised, with a standardised layout of roads and houses, even the size of bricks, it is clear that they were home to diverse communities that followed different funeral practices. Sometimes bodies were buried, at other times they were cremated, or their bones were buried in pots, and sometimes, in what may have been symbolic burial, pots were buried without any bones.

In Dholavira, in the arid lands of Kutch, is an ancient Harappan site, where the city is built using stones, not fire-baked bricks as in the Indus Valley cities. What is unique about this site is that it has a vast cemetery of cenotaphs—burial sites with no dead bodies. Instead, there are stones to indicate coffins. Were these built to honour traders who never returned from their mercantile mission? We do not know.

Dolmens

In South India, we find vast fields of menhirs and dolmens belonging to the Megalithic (big stone) Iron Age, dating to around 1000 BCE. Giant stones were erected to mark the burial site. Sometimes five large flat stones have been arranged to create a room with a floor and a roof held up by three walls. The southern wall is usually missing, which has led to the suggestion that the idea of equating the southern direction with the dead may have been adopted by Vedic Aryans who married women from such communities. This is speculation, of course. We have no details of what these practices might have been. What we are fairly sure of is that rebirth was not a dominant idea.

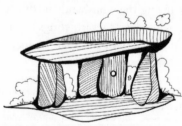

Dolmen raised to the dead in the Iron Age

We can speculate, however, that the ancients believed that ghosts lingered in a realm of spirits that co-existed with the realm of the living. Offerings of food and clothes, lamps and incense were made at these dolmen sites. In Buddhist literature, we come across tales of monks who ate the food or took the clothes meant for the dead from burial sites outside the village, angering spirits who then followed them to their monasteries.

The dead could occasionally be summoned by special ritualists, who would wear special costumes, prepare their body with fasting, dance and make music until the spirit entered their body and spoke through them to the community, resolving issues, expressing concern and communicating good news. The practice continues today as the Bhuta-daivam and Theyyam practices found in Tulunadu in south Karnataka and north Kerala.

Samadhi

When the Buddha died, his body was cremated. His followers fought over his bones. These were carried to several places across India and buried around large mounds (stupa) that became objects of veneration. Thus rose the belief that the power of a great man outlived his death wherever his remains were kept. In the Buddhist tradition, we find stupas and pagodas, where the remains of great teachers (arhat) are placed.

Since Brahmins and Buddhists were rivals, the former pejoratively referred to the latter as worshippers of bones. However, Hindu monastic orders (matha) continue the practice of burial mounds in the form of samadhi shrines for their leaders.

Even though Buddhism waned in India, monastic practices and monastic orders continued in the region, now led by Hindu leaders, experts in Vedanta and yoga. Like Buddhist teachers, the heads of matha

Stupa is a burial mound
containing the relics
of the Buddha

Hindu holy men are
buried in the seated
position; a sacred tulsi
plant is grown on the
site above

Samadhi is a mound
marking the site where a
holy man chose death and
voluntarily released his spirit
from his flesh

continue to be buried in a seated position. It is believed that their body is pure, as they have mastered yoga and can voluntarily cause their spirit to leave their body through the practice of samadhi. They would never be reborn, and so there is no need for the usual Vedic funeral rituals of cremation and feeding.

The body is buried in seated position in a pit filled with salt. Salt hastens dehydration, and prevents the smell of rotting flesh from attracting carnivores. The skull is cracked open with a coconut, to ensure the preta leaves the body. The burial site is marked by a plant or a tree, usually tulsi but sometimes the banyan. In many mathas of India, there is a special compound where one finds clusters of the 'samadhi' of old teachers.

Viragal

Hero memorial stone from Rajasthan

In the Deccan region, wooden pillars and stones are raised in memory of the dead, usually ancestors or warriors who died protecting the land and cattle from wild animals, invaders and thieves. Between the third and the sixteenth centuries, we find elaborately carved panels across the Konkan, Karnataka, Andhra and Tamil Nadu that commemorate a hero (vira) who died a violent death. These 'hero stones' or 'hero steles' are called 'viragal'.

The lowermost panel of the carving depicts the reason for death, the middle panel shows the deceased's journey to the celestial realms and the top panel portrays the deity whose heaven welcomes the hero. Eternity is indicated by the symbol of the sun and moon. The deity can be Shiva, Vishnu, Lakshmi or even a Jain Tirthankara. The reason for death is usually a

Viragal or hero stones from South India

Devdutt Pattanaik

battle or attack by a wild animal (tiger, boar, leopard).

Sometimes the hero beheads himself or rips out his own entrails to express his devotion to a chieftain. The hero could also be a woman who chooses to burn herself to express her devotion to her husband.

The stones were bathed with water and milk, anointed with sandal paste and turmeric, and offered fruits and flowers and animal sacrifices, to ensure the spirit of the dead brought security and prosperity to the community. The worship of such hero stones was probably a forerunner to the temple culture that Hinduism embraced about 1,500 years ago.

Sepulcher Shrine

A thousand years ago, when great Chola kings died, their burial or cremation spots were marked by a Shiva-linga called 'pallippadai'. The shrines received royal patronage. The king's identity was merged with that of Shiva and the two powers, royal and divine, were invoked through prayer and ritual to bestow prosperity and security to the land.

Votive Shiva-linga placed above royal burial or cremation sites to mark the union of the deceased with Shiva

The sun and moon symbols were intended to show that the living wanted the memory of the king to last for eternity.

These shrines were probably popularised by followers of the Kalamukha and Kapalika schools of Shaivism. This practice of creating shrines to the dead was later frowned upon because death was seen as inauspicious and bones were seen as carriers of impurity. With time, the practice was abandoned, and memories of such shrines were actively erased as Brahmin orthodoxy introduced the idea of death being a source of impurity and inauspiciousness.

Chhatri

Chattri raised in memory of a Rajput king at the site of a royal cremation

Nowadays, when a political leader is cremated, a shrine is built to mark the spot. It is called a 'samadhi', but is in fact a 'chhatri', or pavilion, a practice that was popularised by the Rajput kings during the Mughal era. The sites where Rajput kings died, or were cremated, were often marked by hero stones. But during the Mughal era, the Rajputs began building grand pavilions to mark the spot, perhaps imitating the Mughals who were building elaborate tombs for their fallen warriors and leaders.

The practice began after the Delhi Sultans adopted the custom of building mausoleums for their fathers, imitating a Persian tradition. The royal chhatri was one way to reintroduce Hindu architecture since building temples with spires (shikhara) was discouraged by the Sultans.

Chhatri—umbrella—has long been associated with royalty in India. A king is supposed to be the umbrella that shelters his people. Later, the structures became so elaborate that they resembled temples. The purpose was to establish the authority of the royal clan, and to connect the current generation of kings with their great past. It was meant to constantly remind people how the current power of kings came from past greatness. Here, memory mattered for political reasons, even if it was in contravention of the Vedic belief that memory prevents the preta from making its journey to Pitr-loka.

Chapter 4

Women of the Dead

In which we learn how the life and death of the husband determines the status of Hindu women as sadhava, vidhava, nityasumangali and sati maharani

The Harappan civilisation is known for its bangles made of shell and bones and clay. Women here wore bangles more than women in any other known civilisation. Similar bangles are worn by young married women even today. It is the symbol of being a sadhava, a married woman whose husband is alive. When a woman loses her husband, she breaks her bangles and is declared a widow, a vidhava. In folk superstition, the sight of a sadhava is said to bring good luck while that of a vidhava is said to bring bad luck.

This division between the married woman and the widow is first documented in the Rig Veda (10.18.7), 'Women who are not widows, who have good husbands, who have no tears in their eyes, no sorrow or sickness, let them anoint their eyes with cream, and well-adorned step into the marriage bed. She who lies beside the man whose breath is gone, let her rise and return to the world of living to the man who desires her and holds her hand.' Here, the vidhava who is asked to lie beside her husband's corpse is probably raised by the man who grasps her hand in public, remarries her and restores her status as sadhava.

The Harappan civilisation thrived over 4,000 years ago in and around the Indus valley. The Vedic civilisation developed some 3,000 years ago in and around the Gangetic plains. The Vedas speaks of wars between kings. The epic Mahabharata perhaps retains memories of these battles.

The bedecked bride and the widow shorn of all finery

In the Mahabharata's Stri Parva, we have images of war widows wailing, beating their chest, undoing their hair, rolling on the ground and throwing dust on their faces. The imagery became increasingly tragic and macabre.

The Tamil Sangam culture flourished about 2,000 years ago in the southern part of India. In Sangam poetry, we hear the earliest wailings of widows, their misery at the loss of a husband and repeated reference to the 'unbangled arms' of the widow and the 'bangled arms' of the married woman. This is probably when sadhava started being seen as auspicious and the vidhava as inauspicious. It is in Sangam literature that we first find the idea of a woman's power being enhanced by her sexuality, her marriage, her fidelity. In the story of Kannagi, when her husband is wrongly killed by the king, the angry chaste wife has the power to set the kingdom aflame.

Sadhava

In the Ramayana, when Ram is going to the forest with Sita, he removes his royal robes and wears those of a hermit. Sita, however, is prevented from removing her ornaments. In the forest, Arundhati, wife of Vasishtha, gives her special robes that will never get dirty. A woman whose husband is alive must always be adorned. Her happiness brings good luck to the family.

When Ravana abducts her, Sita removes all her jewellery and drops it on the floor, an indicator of the loss of auspiciousness. She sits in Lanka unhappy and unadorned, and so brings misfortune to that city of gold. Similar misfortune comes to Hastinapur when Draupadi, the daughter-in-law of the royal household (kula-vadhu), is dragged by the hair and disrobed in public.

In sacred Hindu rituals, a woman with a husband and child(ren) is called 'sumangali', the lucky one who brings luck wherever she goes. Such women are seen in this context as priestesses of the household, who turned the house into a home. They perform vratas, or observances, that involve fasting and praying to attract fortune to the house, and also adorn their body and their homes. Rituals like haldi-kumkum, Mangala-Gauri in Maharashtra, Gangaur in Rajasthan, Teej in the Gangetic plains, and Sindoor-khela in Bengal are still celebrated, where married women with children gather to celebrate each other's auspicious womanhood. Women are identified with Gauri, the domestic form of Shakti, the wife of Shiva.

The act of beautification, shringara, is extended to the house, which is decorated with floral strings at the gateway (torana), paintings on the wall (alpana) and the floor (rangoli, kolam). The bride is considered a diminutive double of Lakshmi, wife of Vishnu. Her entry into the household, after marriage, is announced with conch-shell trumpets. To see her face is to invite good luck. Her footprint and palm print are considered auspicious, holding the promise of abundance and growth.

Vidhava

In the Ramayana, we learn of Vali's widow, Tara, marrying his brother, Sugriva, and Ravana's widow, Mandodari, marrying his brother, Vibhishana. This enables the brothers to inherit their elder brother's throne. In the Mahabharata, however, the two widows of Vichitravirya are not allowed to remarry. Instead, a sage is asked to make them pregnant. The children thus born are considered Vichitravirya's children.

The wife is described as the field that belongs to the husband; any man can sow the seed in this field, but the children belong to the husband. Thus, we see in the Mahabharata the woman being seen as a property of her husband. The Pandavas are children of Pandu even though their mothers are made pregnant by the gods. It is an indication of the changing status of women.

This change was closely connected with property and inheritance. In patrilineal families, where children and all property belonged to the husband, remarriage was forbidden to ensure that the property stayed within the deceased husband's household. Widows who had no children were then seen as a liability, an extra mouth to feed. However, in matrilineal clans, where property passed on to the woman's children, it did not matter who the husband was, so women could have many lovers.

The sadhava–vidhava divide was far more common amongst the elite. In families without wealth and property to inherit, women were free to remarry. However, in affluent families, there was a dramatic ceremony dreaded by women that followed the death of a husband—the vermillion mark on a woman's forehead and the parting in her hair (sindoor) was wiped off, her bangles were broken, as was the marriage thread (mangalsutra), her head was shaved and she was made to wear white clothes. The ceremony was meant to strip the woman of all status and pleasure. The situation was worse if the widow had no children.

In medieval times, when women were seen as totally dependent on fathers and husbands, a vidhava was seen as bringing bad luck and misfortune. Unadorned and wearing white, she was not to eat salt or spices. She had to spend her time in isolation, praying to God. She was not allowed to participate in festivities or fertility rites such as marriage and childbirth. Sometimes, she was abandoned, forced to fend for herself in the temple towns of Kashi and Mathura, praying to the gods and depending on alms.

Such was the low status of the widow in traditional Hindu society, especially in the elite upper strata. It was a world away from that of the Rig Vedic hymn, where a widow re-enters the world of the living with a new husband who desires her and holds her hand. Calls to end child marriage and promote widow remarriage led to the Hindu Reformation of the nineteenth century, though some saw this as an assault to traditional Indian values.

Sati Maharani

The widow who burnt herself voluntarily on her husband's funeral pyre was venerated as a goddess in many parts of India and was known as 'Sati Maharani'. Across India, we find sati stones to commemorate such an event. These stones are worshipped for good luck.

Stories of Indian women immolating themselves on their husband's funeral pyre recur in the writings of the ancient Greeks as well as the medieval Arabic and European travellers. It was a popular practice among warrior clans, especially the Rajputs, but was also practised in some royal families of the Deccan regions. And it became popular amongst Bengali Brahmin communities in the nineteenth century, leading to the East India Company passing laws to outlaw sati.

Sati stone marking the site of widow burning, a practice once common in warrior communities

The word 'sati' denotes a woman who is totally faithful to her husband, a quality that is supposed to give her magical powers, attract good luck and even the ability to withstand the heat of fire. In the Ramayana, being faithful to Ram gives Sita the power to walk through fire. However, over time, the word 'sati' came to denote the widow who joined her husband in death, determined to walk together in the land of the dead.

Significantly, this infamous practice has no sanction in any religious literature, from the Vedas to the Dharma-shastra. But we find it mentioned in the Mahabharata, when Pandu's widow Madri kills herself on his pyre, as do some of the wives of Krishna. The oldest Sanskrit Ramayana, some 2,000 years old, has no reference to sati, but in the regional Telugu version of the epic, which is 500 years old, Sulochana performs sati holding the corpse of her husband, Ravana's son Meghanad.

Mirabai, the Rajput princess who lived five centuries ago, was constantly harassed by her husband's family because she refused to immolate herself on her husband's funeral pyre and chose instead to worship Krishna in Vrindavan. The cruel treatment meted out to widows could have been why the idea of immolating themselves on the funeral pyre seemed like a good alternative for many Hindu widows. The practice is now banned by law in the Republic of India.

Nityasumangali

In Tamil epics, we find three kinds of women. There is the nun, attached to no man, who sought freedom from the wheel of rebirths. There was the chaste, faithful wife, the Pattini of Tamil lore, the Sati of Sanskrit lore, who walked with her husband in life and in death over seven lifetimes. Finally, the courtesan, attached to many men, who enjoyed the eternal pleasures of paradise.

Courtesans were referred to as 'nityasumangali', the eternal bride, women who never become widows, as they have many husbands. They never mourned like widows; there was always a husband, a provider, for them. The courtesans or ganika were considered auspicious, and were thus invited to wedding, childbirth and housewarming ceremonies. They were asked to tie the wedding thread of the bride and bless her with luck. The nityasumangali was linked to luxury, hospitality and pleasure. Her wealth and skills were passed on from mother to daughter.

In the Atharva Veda, fickle fortune was connected to courtesans as well as the game of dice, and also to Lakshmi, the whimsical, restless goddess of fortune and pleasure. The courtesans were earthly counterparts of the apsaras of Swarga. They provide pleasure to all but belong to none.

In medieval times, these women were married to temple gods. Since gods are immortal, these women could never be widows. They could go to any man, as God is present in all men. Temple inscriptions from the sixth and the tenth centuries indicate hundreds of women dedicated to temples in Odisha, Gujarat, Kashmir, Andhra, Goa and Tamil Nadu. They were all linked to music and dance.

None of these women was shunned in the older Hindu imagination. However, during colonial rule, courtesans were deemed to be prostitutes, their vocation was considered impure and illegal and they were wiped out from society and erased from history.

Devdutt Pattanaik

Chapter 5

Caretakers of the Dead

In which we learn about how the caste system and the practice of untouchability is intimately related to the Hindu idea that death is inauspicious and impure

Daksha, the Brahmin patriarch, shunned the crematorium. There wandered Shiva, in the company of dogs and ghosts. Daksha's daughter chose Shiva as her husband much to Daksha's irritation. Daksha refused to invite Shiva to yagna and offer him food. An enraged Sati killed herself by jumping in her father's fire altar. Daksha remained indifferent. In fury, Shiva attacked the yagna-shala and beheaded Daksha. The Devas, who needed the yagna to feed themselves, begged Shiva to restore the yagna. Shiva gave Daksha a goat's head, who has since ensured that all leftovers (ucchista) would belong to Shiva and his people. From that day, Shiva and Shakti became part of both Vedic and Tantric worship. In the left-hand path, Shiva and Shakti take the form of the fierce Bhairava and Bhairavi, while in right-hand path they take the form of the gentle Shankara and Gauri. This story explains the two paths of Hinduism: the purity-conscious right-hand path (dakshina marga, or Veda), and the impurity-embracing left-hand path (vama marga, or Tantra).

Impurity was a source of knowledge and power for the Aghori, but it rendered the Chandala inauspicious. Chandala was the one whose hereditary occupation it was to clear the village of dead bodies and tend to funeral pyres. The exclusion of the Chandala from the village on grounds of purity, referred to in late Vedic scriptures, is one of the earliest examples of the practice of untouchability.

Chandala

In the Puranas, Swarga is located above the sky and Naraka below the earth. Swarga is full of pleasures, and Naraka full of pain. Swarga is for those who fed the gods when alive, Naraka for those who fed no one when alive. Swarga is for the Devas, who do not fear death. Naraka is for the preta, who yearn to be reborn. Swarga is full of purity, joy and auspiciousness. Naraka is full of impurity, sorrow and inauspiciousness.

This cosmic architecture manifests in the ideal of the Hindu settlement. In the centre is the temple, attracting all things beautiful and good (mangala), managed by Vedic priests who follow strict rules of purity. In the periphery of the village is the crematorium, impure and inauspicious (amangala), where live those who dispose of the corpses, the Chandala.

It is theorised that this superimposition of the cosmic architecture on the village played a key role in the rise of the caste system, with 'higher pure' communities located centrally around the temple and 'lower impure' communities marginalised socially, physically and psychologically. Entry into caste was determined by birth and escape by death.

The so-called 'untouchable' Chandala, wearing animal hide, followed by dogs, carrying a spitoon, with bells on his staff to announce his arrival and a broom to wipe his footprints

Late Vedic texts, such as the Chandogya Upanishad, over 2,500 years old, mention the Chandala. We also learn of his life from the writings of Chinese monks who came to India to study Buddhism 1,500 years ago. The Chandala lived in the crematorium and tended to funeral pyres. He ate whatever was offered to the dead, and wore clothes gifted to the dead. Skulls and bones became his utensils and tools. The dogs that roamed the crematorium were his companions. His presence was considered inauspicious, his shadow was shunned.

The association of death with impurity is why the crematorium is always located outside the village. Those who enter the crematorium become temporarily

Devdutt Pattanaik

impure, and must bathe when they return home. Brahmins who perform funeral rituals, and receive gifts as stand-ins for the dead, are considered to be of lower status too. Those whose family vocation it was to tend to the funeral pyres, and so had to live around the crematorium, were considered the most impure of communities, shunned by the village.

Over centuries, as notions of purity were elaborated, the Chandalas were placed lower and lower in the expanding and evolving caste hierarchy. It fell to them to clear the village of dead bodies of those without families as well as the dead bodies of animals. As the Chandala was seen as a source of pollution, the only fire he was allowed access to was the funeral fire. The only water he was allowed access to was the water used in funeral rituals. In its extreme form, the caretakers of the dead had to carry a pot around their neck so that their spit never touched the village ground. They had to carry a broom to wipe out their footprints. They had to wear bells so that their approach could be heard from a distance, giving people a chance to avoid their sight and shadow.

The Chandala is associated with Shiva in many stories. Shiva too wanders the crematorium, adorns himself with skulls and bones, smears his body with ash and is connected to the dogs of the cremation ground in his Bhairava form. There are stories where Shiva comes in the form of a Chandala and offers Amrita to sages in a cup fashioned from a skull. The sages shun the Chandala's shadow, refuse the drink and thus lose a chance at immortality. In Tantric circles, stories such as these make the Chandala an object of veneration due to his association with death, looking at the wisdom that a familiarity with death would grant him.

The Bhairava form of Shiva is linked to Brahmin-killing or Brahma-hatya because Shiva beheads Brahma as well as Daksha. Brahma chases after his daughter, a metaphor for attachment. Daksha controls his daughter, a metaphor for insecurity. By beheading them, Shiva introduces the idea of tapa, the fire of restraint that burns cravings. Shiva is called 'Kapalika' as he carries the Brahma's skull everywhere. He teaches the doctrine of atma, reminding all creatures to look beyond pure and impure vocations, and recognise the soul in all bodies. His consort, Chamunda, also known as Bhairavi, sits on corpses, bedecks herself with the heads and limbs of the dead, eats flesh and rides on ghosts. This puts the Bhairava and the Bhairavi in direct conflict with the purity-seeking Brahmin. They are equated with the ucchista in Vedic lore. A leftover from the pre-Vedic ways when death was venerated not feared, when the crematorium was where you went to learn. It was an idea that inspired the folk tales of a king called Vikramaditya who tries to catch a ghost, a vetala, that resided in a crematorium.

In the Puranic story of Raja Harishchandra, the king becomes so poor that, to pay ritual fees to Rishi Vishwamitra, he has to sell himself and his wife. His wife becomes slave to a Brahmin family, where she is constantly abused. He becomes slave to a Chandala, where he is treated with respect. Yet, his fate is considered worse than hers. He accepts his fate stoically, earning the respect of the gods, who elevate him to the status of Indra, king of Swarga. The Chandala and the cremation ground are thus deeply intertwined with the secret knowledge and occult ideas of Tantra.

These stories, however, did not elevate the status of the Chandala or loosen the stranglehold of Brahminical notions of purity. The Chandala remained the outsider, and contact with him was always considered transgressive by 'upper' castes.

Aghori

Vedic culture was initially confined to the upper Gangetic plains. In the rest of the subcontinent, tribes and other local communities buried their dead and did not believe in rebirth. Stones were raised to mark the spot of burial. Kings and warriors who died in conflict defending the community were venerated as heroes. Musicians played drums and sang songs of their glory. Shamans donned masks and make-up and bright clothes to invoke the spirits of the ancestors and invite the pitr to occupy their body temporarily and speak to the living, guide them and resolve disputes. To make their body worthy, the shamans would fast, denying it the pleasure of sleep and food. These practices are found today in south Karnataka and north Kerala in the form of Bhuta-kolam (dance of Bhuta-daivam) and Theyyam rituals, performed by members at the lower rung of the caste hierarchy, rendered divine during the period of the ritual, which invariably takes place at night.

In these communities, the spirits of the ancestors were the earliest gods known to the common folk. They lived amongst the living—feared, respected, venerated. This was the Bhuta-loka, or the invisible realm of the ghosts, ever-present and readily accessible to special performer priests. It was the realm of Bhairava and Bhairavi.

Buddhist lore is full of yaksha spirits in the crematorium who trouble monks who eat food offered to them. These bhutas were sometimes offered food in Buddhist monasteries. These stories indicate beliefs and practices before the popularity of Vedic rituals. Across India today there are shaman-like priests who can talk to spirits and communicate the will of ancestors. There are even those who still wander in crematoriums, looking for the corpses of the dead, seeking wisdom from ghosts. They are called Aghori, the ones who must not be feared. Perhaps they owe their origin to pre-Vedic or extra-Vedic customs and beliefs.

Vedic priests considered these practices inauspicious and impure, and encouraged people to perform antyeshti and shradh so that the spirit of the dead could travel across Vaitarni to await rebirth, and thus another chance at liberation from rebirth. The body had to be cremated so that its bones and skull could not be used by Aghoris in secret occult rituals involving corpses (shava-sadhana). The crematorium (where the dead are burnt or cast into rivers), the cemetery (where the dead are buried) and the charnel ground (where bodies are exposed to air) were in the Vedic imagination a place haunted by dark, mysterious, dangerous and negative forces. They even shunned the Chandala, connecting with him only during the time of death.

The Vedic world valued the mantra, from the word 'manas', or mind. In the early Vedic world, 'manas' was one of the many words used for spirit, the others being jiva, atma, asu and prana. The Tantric world valued tanu, the body. While the Vedic world sought to help the preta make the journey to the world of the ancestors, the Tantric world figured out ways by which the atma could leave the flesh voluntarily: a practice called 'samadhi' in yoga. The atma could then travel to the world of spirits and gods and return to the body at will. These practices are referred to in early yoga texts. The Tantrics also figured out how an individual yogi's jiva-atma could merge with the cosmic param-atma; this formed the

Shava-sadhana or rituals involving corpses

Tantric Mahasiddha in a charnel ground where bodies are left to rot

basis of Hindu mysticism. They figured out how the jiva-atma could be energised by the kundalini, the untapped force of the flesh, so that an individual can bloom and acquire supernatural powers, siddha, such as flying in air, walking on water, changing shape and size, manipulating space and time. This was Hindu occult. The experts of the occult were called Nath in North India and Siddha in South India.

The word 'shaman' is sometimes traced to the Shramana, Buddhist and Jain monks who chose meditation and breathing practices over Vedic fire rituals. Often, these monks lived outside the village, in the forest, atop mountains, and engaged with those who lived in the crematorium. They had no problem eating food or wearing clothes that had been given to the ancestors. They engaged with the dead, and with caretakers of the dead. This played a key role in the growth of the Tantric schools of Buddhism, Jainism and Hinduism.

Tantric gurus of Vajrayana Buddhism, such as Padmasambhava, and many of the eighty-four Siddha are shown holding skulls and bones, and residing in charnel grounds surrounded by rotting corpses. Only the brave approached them. The Adi Guru, or primal teacher of the Nath, known as Datta, is depicted with dogs and a cow alongside him, balancing the Tantric and the Vedic ways, living on the edge of the village under a banyan tree.

The attempt to make Tantra a part of the mainstream was led by Adi Shankara, who in the seventh century popularised Vedic culture across tribes and communities. He was born in a Brahmin family. His father died young, and he was brought up by a mother who nurtured his independent spirit. He saw the limitations of Brahmin rituals of exclusion and the value of the Buddhist practices of inclusion. Adi Shankara decided that there was more value in connecting communities than disconnecting them. He saw the overlaps between the Buddhist idea of shunya (nothingness) and the Hindu idea of nirguna (formless divine). In Shiva's endless pillar of fire (jyotir-linga), he identified the form of the formless divine.

Against the wishes of his mother, he became a sanyasi. However, breaking the code of Vedic samskara, Adi Shankara returned to perform his mother's funeral rites. In other words, though a hermit who technically has no family, he performed his duty as a son. This was transgressive. He clearly saw greater value in formless meaning than in language, in the idea more than the ritual, the soul more than the flesh.

Adi Shankara came from Kerala, where the old secret rituals of summoning ancestral spirits into the bodies of the living continues. He engaged with a Chandala man, as we know from one of his encounters in Kashi. Adi Shankara asked a Chandala to move away from his path. The Chandala said, 'You want me to move or my soul to move? But did you not say the soul is everywhere? So how can it be moved? And if everything is the soul, why do you ask me to move?' These words so impressed the scholar that he was convinced the Chandala was Shiva in disguise.

From Adi Shankara's biography, composed nearly five centuries after his time, we learn about his knowledge of parakaya pravesh, the occult practice of leaving one's body and experiencing life through another man's body. He valued the hermit's life over the householder's, which led to some people accusing him of wrapping Buddhist concepts in Hindu clothing. A woman called Ubhaya Bharati asked him about his knowledge of Tantra and Kama-shastra—knowledge of the body and experience of sex and other sensual pursuits. How would a hermit who had taken a vow of celibacy and restraint experience this knowledge? Adi Shankara is then said to have practised an occult ritual. He went into the yogic state of samadhi that allows the yogi to voluntarily separate the atma from the sharira, the soul from the body, and slip out like a sword leaving a scabbard. He then entered the dead body of a king called Amaru. The king's corpse got reanimated, and through Amaru's body, in his pleasure palace, Adi Shankara experienced all kinds of physical pleasures. This led him to compose *Amaru Shataka*, a Sanskrit work on sensual delights.

Parakaya pravesh or the Tantric occult practice of leaving one's body and inhabiting a corpse to experience life through another body

Tantric practice enabled Adi Shankara to maintain the purity of his flesh, yet experience what the Vedic world deemed impure. He is venerated by both Vedantins as well as Tantrics. His access to Tantra helped him voluntarily nudge his jiva-atma out of his body, and his knowledge of Vedanta helped him appreciate that the jiva-atma is no different from the param-atma, the cosmic soul. Adi Shankara is, therefore, a great teacher of mysticism as well as of occult, samadhi as well as siddhi. Mysticism unites the jiva-atma to the param-atma. Occult gets the jiva-atma energised by the kundalini so that it is no longer limited by the flesh and has access to supernatural powers. Together, there was more to learn about life. Inclusion was the key, not exclusion.

Devdutt Pattanaik

Chapter 6

Fear of the Dead

In which we learn about bhuta, preta,
pishacha, vetala and other ghosts described in
the occult traditions of India

There's a popular trope in Hollywood films, of soulless zombies who walk around eating the living, infecting them. And there are the vampires, immortal but not alive, undead and craving human blood. In other movies, we've met demons from hell who rise up to torment the living, and ghosts who were not buried in holy ground and so wander in the woods, haunting homes and possessing humans. The exorcist is called upon to drive them out of our earth to purgatory and back to hell. They fear Christian religious symbols and verses from the Bible because they are based on the Christian mythological universe, and also based on the concept of only one life.

In the Indian cultural context, these ideas make no sense, for Indian ghosts belong to a different mythological universe—one based on rebirth, where there is no concept of evil (something outside God), where the charnel ground (smashan-bhoomi) of cremation and burial is a place of wisdom too. Many Tantric practices take place in the crematorium and involve dead bodies and the spirits of the dead. According to the Garuda Purana, unless a Brahmin performs the antyeshti and shradh ceremonies, the preta will not be able to cross the Vaitarni and become a pitr. He will remain trapped in the world of living, and that is not good. As bhutas, they torment the living. As pishachas, they torment the dead. As vetala, they are tormented by sorcerers.

The ghosts of Hinduism are lost and trapped, not evil. While there are rituals to drive away ghosts, they acknowledge the hunger and attachment of these tragic souls. The point of Hindu exorcism is to facilitate movement. This may involve mock rage, threats, compassionate cajoling, even bribes, with promises to resolve every issue that prevents the dead from moving on. Hanuman, who went to Patala and rescued Ram and Lakshman from demons, is often invoked for protection, as all ghosts fear Hanuman and see him as an aspect of Shiva-Bhairava.

Preta

After death, and funeral rituals, the spirit of the dead, that is, the preta, lives in the crematorium for a few days before it can make its journey across the Vaitarni to Yama-loka. During this period, it is lost and frightened and so compassionate relatives comfort it with a lamp, some water and even germinating seeds. The Garuda Purana states that those who died while travelling, away from home, in accidents, or during epidemics and famine also wait in crematoriums hoping that their family members remember them and perform the requisite rituals. Until this is done, they cannot go to the land of the dead. Trapped on the wrong side, they torment the living, haunting them and possessing them, until rituals are performed to get them to go. In Kashi, there are songs where it is said that Shiva plays Holi every day in the cremation ground with ash instead of colour with resident ghosts. Most ghosts are temporary residents and eventually make their way to Yama's realm. But some stay back and create trouble for the living.

The preta are typically imagined as hiding amongst the aerial roots of the banyan tree. They hang upside down like bats on the tree, as the pitr do in Yama-loka. The banyan tree is, therefore, not a householder's plant; only hermits seek its shade. Shiva is often shown as seated under a banyan tree, teaching hermits the secret of atma. Vishnu takes the form of a baby and floats on a banyan leaf that is being cradled and tossed by the waters of doom and death (pralaya). Both Shiva and Vishnu comfort the preta, urging them to not lose hope.

We gather from local lore that ghosts are of two types: those eager to cross to the other side, and those who are not. The reluctant ghosts include those who are still attached to the land of the living, clinging to family and fortune or to emotions such as rage, jealousy, vengeance and injustice.

The funeral rituals prescribed in the Garuda Purana are meant to calm them down, just as food calms those who are hungry and angry. Public ceremonies are encouraged for the dead so that even strangers, the nameless forgotten dead, beggars, orphans and widows, those whose rituals have not been performed, may find peace. All is well only after the preta reaches the land of the dead and becomes a pitr.

There is a fascinating story from the Sanskrit collection of tales known as *Kathasaritsagar* that speaks of the anxiety of the preta even after becoming pitr. A king was conducting his annual pinda-daan when three hands rose from the earth to receive the offerings. One belonged to a Brahmin, one to a Kshatriya and one to a Vaishya. The man who married the king's mother was a Vaishya, but the man who made her pregnant was a Brahmin, and the man who raised him was a Kshatriya. So, who was the real father? Who should get the offering? The answer to this question depends on various legal and social criteria. But the king decided that all the dead, whether related or not, should receive offerings. That generosity is the hallmark of a great king.

The hungry hands of the dead as per many folk tales

Bhuta

The word 'bhuta' has many meanings. Bhuta denotes the elements: air, fire, water, earth and ether. The 'past' is another meaning of the word. It means 'ghost' too. Bhuta refers to ghosts who cling to the past because no ceremony has been performed to help them travel to the future. They are trapped in the land of the living without a body. So, they haunt the living, taking refuge in lonely spots and abandoned homes.

In many communities, the bhuta is summoned through ritual to bless the living, reveal the future and resolve disputes. The summoning is

Bhuta dhaivam of Tulu Nadu is an ancestor spirit who communicates with the living through special priests who prepare their bodies by fasting and wearing the ritual dress. They go into trance with music and dance.

done by specially trained shamans who sing, dance and make music. They prepare their body with paints and masks to serve as a vessel for the spirit. In Kerala, these ritual performances are called Theyyam (Daivam, 'god' in Sanskrit) which refers to gods.

In Tulu Nadu, south Karnataka, this ritual performance is called Bhuta-kolam. The spirits thus summoned could be of great men and women, who were powerful leaders, and fought wild animals and invaders. Their power is invoked to serve the living. The bhuta is not feared here; he is revered. In many farms of Kerala and Tulu Nadu, special shrines are built in their honour. They are given their favourite food, which includes meat and toddy.

The most common meaning of bhuta remains a ghost who troubles the living. A ghost for whom funeral rites have not been performed makes his unhappiness felt in many ways: accidents, diseases, misfortune, miscarriages, diseased cattle, rotting of food, foul smell, nightmares, moving objects, hallucinations, hysteria. When buildings and bridges keep falling people fear the presence of unhappy spirits. So rituals are performed to feed and calm and reassure the dead.

But there are ghosts who do not want to cross the Vaitarni. They are still attached to the life lived and seek revenge or justice. They long for the life they had or lost. This is moha or attachment. With no sense of time, they stick around on earth long after their loved ones are dead.

Pishacha

If Devas fear Asuras, if rishis fear rakshasas, then the preta and the pitr fear the pishacha. The preta becomes a pitr because he has family. But when a preta has no family to help it turn into a pitr, it becomes a pishacha, a tormentor of the dead. It also torments the living—frightening people, driving people mad, polluting water and fire, spoiling food, filling the house with foul odours, causing the body to break into boils and rashes,

Devdutt Pattanaik

twisting tongues so that people say foul and mean things, destroying relationships, causing miscarriages and accidents, causing sheep and goats and cattle to get lost, causing mosquitoes and fleas to spread disease.

However, there are special rituals to help the pishacha calm down and enable its journey to pitr-loka. Sternly but compassionately, it needs to be told to let go and move on.

The earliest reference to ghosts who torment the dead is in the Rig Veda, in the Hymn of Yama, where they are told, 'Go away, get away, crawl away from here. The ancestors have prepared a place for our dead. Yama provides food and resting places for him already.'

Pishacha who torments the preta in the crematorium

Vetala

As per tales first narrated around eighth century CE in Central India, King Vikramaditya was sent by a sorcerer to fetch a vetala from the crematorium for a sorcerer. As long as the king is silent, he can carry the vetala. If he speaks, the vetala will go back to its tree. The vetala does not want to be caught, and so poses puzzles and demands that Vikramaditya solve them to prove that he is indeed the great Vikramaditya and not an imposter, thus teasing the king's royal ego. He also warns the king that his head will split if he knows the answer and refuses to answer. Vikramaditya succumbs twenty-four times. The twenty-fifth time, Vikramaditya is relieved, for he does not know the answer and stays silent. The vetala laughs and says that the ignorance of the king will cost him dearly. The sorcerer will use

Vikramaditya and vetala which probably inspired, or was inspired by, the tale of Solomon (Suleiman) and his djinn

the vetala in a Tantric ritual to gain powers that will help him overthrow Vikramaditya himself.

This collection of folk tales known as the *Vetala-pachisi* or twenty-five tales of the vetala is an indication of how important sorcery was in royal courts of early medieval India, and also of the relationship of sorcery with the dead. Vetala is a ghost that is unable to cross the Vaitarni. Unable to become a pitr, it remains a preta that seeks a body. This is why it occupies corpses, animating them partially, speaking through them, but unable to restore the body to life. The vetala was believed to be the source of great power and wisdom, living as he did in the world of spirits, with access to forbidden knowledge that is unavailable to the living and the dead.

Later in the story, the vetala helps Vikramaditya defeat the sorcerer and becomes his guide. In some versions, the question that Vikramaditya cannot answer is: 'How will you die?' No human knows how they will die, but the vetala, who lives on the border of the land of the living and the land of the dead, can peek into the account books of Chitragupta and reveal their secrets. The vetala is a powerful ally and helps Vikramaditya become a great king. But it too is unable to prevent Vikramaditya's death at the hands of the young potter Shalivahan.

The tale of Vikramaditya's vetala spread to other lands through India's vast trading routes. In Arabia, we learn of a king who is as wise as Vikramaditya, called Suleiman (Solomon), and who has power of djinns, supernatural beings of Arab mythology. Few stories are better known the world over than Aladdin and the genie in the magic lamp.

The word genie comes from djinn, and both ideas are believed to have been inspired by the story of vetala—or conversely, the vetala traces its origins to the djinn. In Persian folklore, God forced the djinn to work for Suleiman because they had become arrogant. The djinn could hear the conversations of the angels and so could predict death. But God decreed they would not predict the death of Suleiman. Suleiman died while seated on the throne while supervising the work of the djinn. Even after he had died, the djinn kept working until termites ate the royal staff of Suleiman and his corpse rolled down his magnificent throne.

Vetala, guardian deity of many villages in Konkan

Devdutt Pattanaik

In many parts of India, such as the Konkan, we find temples dedicated to vetala. They are described as part of Shiva's entourage that accompanied him when he was getting married to the Goddess. They serve as guardians of villages. In Goa, we hear of vetala who walk at night around the village and so are given footwear in gratitude. Vetala typically do not wear clothes and are considered male. They may be remnants of pre-Vedic customs and beliefs.

Brahma-rakshasa

In Indian folklore, a Brahmin who misuses his high position in society can be reduced to a terrifying ghost called Brahma-rakshasa, who is not allowed to cross the Vaitarni unless he makes amends for his misconduct. He has great power but is also a sulky and irritable ghost, yearning for liberation. Bitter and caustic, burdened by his arrogance, he is sometimes worshipped as a deity, one who creates trouble unless acknowledged and fed. This idea of worshipping a troubling spirit is found in Southeast Asia too, where offerings are made to such spirits trapped on the wrong side of the Vaitarni.

The Brahma-rakshasa has to learn detachment. He has to let go of his greed, anger, jealousy and frustration. He has to give away everything he has. He also has to stop seeking food from others. He has to learn to eat his own body. This will transform him into Kirti-mukha, the head of glory, the head of the being who consumes the self rather than the other. The image of a severed head was often seen at the entrance of or atop the roof of temples. Images of giant severed heads are also seen on the top of temples in Cambodia and Indonesia. This is the head of the Brahma-rakshasa if he still seeks food, and the Kirti-mukha if he has outgrown the need for food. In old Tantric temples of Odisha, the severed head symbol is called Vajra-munda, or the diamond head, a reminder of the occult belief that the head is the seat of

Face of Brahma-rakshasa whose terrifying hunger is the result of abusing his privilege when alive. He hurts people until he learns to help.

great wisdom and power. The lolling tongue reminds of his hunger. It mocks our own hunger, encouraging us to outgrow it or end up trapped like a ghost.

These stories underline the importance of Hindu funeral ceremonies and contribute to their widespread popularity across India. They ensured that Brahmins had a role to play in all funeral ceremonies and received gifts as well as fees for services rendered. Stories continuously remind people of the fate of the dead if they are not fed by the living. Their uncremated bodies, their buried skulls and bones will be used in Tantric rituals. Their spirits will be captured and enslaved by sorcerers. So, everyone is encouraged to perform the Vedic ritual of antyeshti, where the body is burnt, the skull is cracked and the bones cast into rivers.

Fear of the dead and the stories they inspire capture the anxieties of the living about the mysterious hereafter.

Devdutt Pattanaik

Chapter 7

History of Death

In which we comprehend how the Hindu understanding
of death has transformed over time, from prehistoric
dolmens and Harappan burials to abbreviated
funeral rituals in electric crematoriums

Contemporary Hindu beliefs and practices can be traced to prehistoric times, Harappa (2500 BCE), Vedic Samhitas (1200 BCE), Brahmana (800 BCE), Srauta-sutra, Grihya-sutra and the Upanishads (500 BCE), the epics Ramayana and the Mahabharata, the Dharma-shastra (300 BCE to 300 CE), the Puranas (post fifth century CE), the Tantras (post tenth century CE) and Bhakti literature (post fifteenth century CE). They even show the influence of Christianity, Islam and modern reform movements.

Prehistoric Times

The shift from animal to human began when humans reflected on death and afterlife and created rituals for the dead. In most Stone Age cultures, we find burial rituals. The dead are sometimes adorned. Their graves are filled with food, clothes, jewellery, weapons and other goods they may need in a future life. Some cremated their dead. Others exposed the body on rocks for birds to eat. Some dunked the body in flowing water. Still others chopped it into pieces which they then cast in rivers, a practice still followed by certain tribes in Northeast India.

Across India, burial sites and pot burial sites have been found in the

Stone Age and Iron Age communities, with menhirs and dolmens raised to honour the dead. Cremation may have been practised too but one would not know, since cremation leaves no record, unless bones and ashes are collected and buried in pots.

Harappan Period

As per archaeologists, the ancient Harappans who built fabulously organised cities around the Indus over 4,000 years ago were the first to grow sesame (til) and crush it to make oil (tel). This was exported to the Middle East. Even today, Hindus offer black sesame seeds to ancestors during Pitr-paksha, the fortnight of the ancestors, while white sesame seeds are offered to the gods (Devas) during festivals like Makara Sankranti, marking the arrival of spring. Sesame oil is lit in ceremonies involving the ancestors, while ghee is lit in ceremonies involving the gods. Through sesame, Hindu culture remains connected to a civilisation that existed over 4,000 years ago.

Harappans used pots in funeral rites. Even today, Hindus use pots in funeral rites to carry the fire that lights the pyre and to carry the water that is poured around the corpse. The pot containing water is symbolically cracked three times to mark the shattering of the body and the release of the spirit.

During rituals, Harappans sat with one knee on the ground, a practice that is still followed while feeding gods and ancestors

Harappans were obsessed with bangles, which even today indicate marital status

Water buffaloes were valued in Harappa. They are mentioned in Rig Veda but linked to Yama only in the Puranas.

Devdutt Pattanaik

Vedic Samhita

The horse was domesticated in 2000 BCE, north of the Black Sea. By 1500 BCE, horse-drawn chariots had reached every corner of the known world—Greece, Turkey, Israel, Egypt, Mesopotamia, Persia, China and India. The Eurasian nomads who brought them to India via Central Asia buried the dead with horses and chariots in Central Asia. However, by the time they had reached the Punjab-Haryana region, around 1500 BCE, and the Rig Veda, after marrying local women, we find hymns that speak of cremation and the journey of ancestors.

In the Atharva Samhita, the last collection of Vedic hymns, we find words for the embodied soul (atma) and the cosmic soul (brahman), and the earliest mention of the metaphor that is repeatedly used in later literature for the human body: 'the lotus flower with nine doors'. The Atharva Veda states that the body results from the contribution of asu by the father and garbha by the mother. These ideas contribute to the incremental Hindu understanding of the body and its origins as elaborated in the Vedanta and Tantra that came much later. The Atharva Veda clearly refers to offering of grain, sesame, milk, ghee and even meat to the deceased and shows veneration for three generations of ancestors. While the Rig Veda focused on bidding farewell to the dead, the Atharva Veda refers to veneration of the dead.

In Rig Samhita, the earliest collection of Vedic hymns, there are hymns that ask fire to gently burn the dead, of ancestors who go on a journey, fear of ghosts who torment the dead and aspiration for a bright imperishable heaven. The word 'svadha' used in rituals related to ancestors is first found here. We also find words that speculate on breath (prana), life (jiva), consciousness (manas) and force (asu). The Rig Veda introduces Yama as the god of the dead, and his four-eyed dogs. There is reference to animals being sacrificed and burnt along with the deceased. The animal thus offered was called anustarani.

In the Rig Veda, there is also reference to the earth who is asked to embrace and comfort the dead like a mother and a sister. There is reference to the idea of returning to nature itself. The breath becomes the wind, the mind becomes the moon, the eyes become the sun. There is talk of regeneration and a new life. The Rig Veda introduces the concepts of Swarga and Naraka, but these are not connected to karma, punishment or rebirth. In all this we see a diversity of beliefs and customs: burials, cremations, collection of bones in urns that are scattered back in nature and a return to a new life in a new body.

Today, during the pinda-daan, tarpan is poured over the pinda, which represents both the flesh and the food of ancestors. The tarpan is water mixed with black sesame, barley and kusha grass. Pinda is made from rice, barley and sesame. Harappan cities used to grow sesame and wheat. Rice came much later, probably from the east. The Rig Veda speaks of barley and kusha grass. This indicates that the funeral rituals today are an amalgamation of many ideas: the pre-Vedic sesame, the Vedic barley and kusha, and the post-Vedic rice.

The mixing of ideas indicates a mixing of cultures. Among the women that the Aryas married, some may have descended from the ancient mercantile cities of the Harappan civilisation, and others from the eastern regions where the dead were buried under mounds. That is why the last verse of the Rig Veda invites all to collaborate.

Brahmana, Srauta-sutra and Grihya-sutra

Early Vedic tradition venerated the collective of ancestors in monthly and annual rites. In later Vedic tradition, the post-funeral shradh rituals of turning the preta into pitr emerged. This developed after 1000 BCE, in the Gangetic plains, and is documented in the Brahmanas. Brahmana literature was composed to elaborately explain the method and logic of various rituals. These were an extension of the Yajur Samhita. Later, public and private ceremonies emerged that were documented in the Srauta-sutra and Grihya-sutra.

The Brahmana literature contains elaborate rituals to recreate the cosmos as the body of the Purusha Prajapati. The cosmos, it says, has sixteen parts, as does the human body. Perhaps, it is from this idea that the ritual of placing sixteen pindas during shradh comes from. Brahmana rituals reveal an obsession with regeneration, renewal and rebirth, and great anxiety related to degeneration, decay and death. They also speak of how all living beings are bound by debts to gods, sages, ancestors, their family and strangers. To repay this debt, humans must perform yagna and the rituals of feeding.

Devdutt Pattanaik

Feeding organisms was ritually done by lighting at least three fires: one for the household, the eastern fire for the gods and the southern fire for ancestors. In Brahmana literature, we find the more elaborate pinda-daan concept—mashed rice or barley balls, mixed with black sesame—being used to represent both the body of the dead and their food. The ancestors are fed along with Agni and

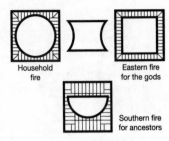

Household fire

Eastern fire for the gods

Southern fire for ancestors

Directions of Vedic altars that have the same meaning today

Soma during the pinda-pitr-yagna on new moon days and during the rainy season ceremonies.

Significantly, Grihya-sutra refers to the collection of bones and ashes after cremation, which are then buried under the ground. This ritual was called pitr-medha. The practice of asthi-visarjan emerged in a later period.

We also find here the tension between the meat-loving priests and the priests who were choosing vegetarian food. The old practice of offering meat of animals to the deceased was being replaced by offering only rice and barley. The Shatapatha Brahmana tells a story to explain the transition. At first, humans were the preferred offering during yagna but their sap entered horses, then bulls, then sheep, then goat and finally earth, from which emerged rice, which was now suitable as food for the gods and ancestors.

Upanishads

By 500 BCE, the Upanishads were being composed. This was after the rise of urban centres in the Gangetic plains, connected by busy trade routes, the use of metal coins (karshapana) as currency by merchants and new ideas such as balance sheet, rebirth and liberation. The Upanishads introduce the idea of the trap of rebirths and the joy of liberation.

In the Katha Upanishad, Yama himself explains to Nachiketa what happens after death: 'If you are enchanted and entrapped by sensory experiences, you will stay trapped in the material world of rebirths. If you can break free from these sensory experiences, you will break free and not be reborn again. Rebirth will trap you in the world of alternating

Yama reveals the secret of death, rebirth and liberation to the child, Nachiketa, in Katha Upanishad

pleasures and pains. Liberation will grant you eternal tranquillity.' To indulge sensory experience is bhoga. The restraining of sensory experiences is yoga. The fire of desire is called kama. The fire that burns kama is called tapa. Here there is no talk of pinda or shradh.

In the Upanishads, the idea of moksha is elaborated as the union of the individual soul with the cosmic soul. This union (yoga) is different from the conceptions of dissolution (nirvana) or isolation (kaivalya) presented by Buddhist and Jain monks at the same time. The monastic orders favoured withdrawal from society, while the Hindu world valued greater engagement with society.

Dharma-shastra

Megasthenes, the Greek ambassador to the Mauryan court spoke of the involvement of Brahmins in the rites of Hades, the Greek counterpart of Yama. He was perhaps referring to the practice of shradh. Texts known as the Dharma-shastra began appearing at this time, from 300 BCE to 300 CE. These works appear to consciously counter Buddhist and Jain precepts of monastic practices that lead to liberation. They value the householder's life instead and advise renunciation only after household obligations have been fulfilled.

Dharma-shastra along with Shrauta-sutra and Grihya-sutra are part of Kalpa-sutra, the corpus of Vedic ceremonies, which is considered a Vedanga, or limb of the Veda. Vedanga, which values ritual and social engagement, was compiled alongside Vedanta, which is more speculative.

By this time, the idea of samsara and samskara were firmly established. Samsara is the realm of karma, applicable to all living organisms who eat and are eaten. Samskara is the realm of dharma, the rituals and cultural practices, and rites of passage that distinguish humans from animals and plants. It is based not on eating and being eaten but on feeding and being fed. The Dharma-shastra further explore the idea introduced in

Devdutt Pattanaik

Brahmana literature that all humans are obliged to repay debts to gods, sages, ancestors and humans by performing yagna. Great value is placed on the shradh rituals.

The Dharma-shastra introduces the idea of feeding Brahmins during the shradh. They are said to represent the ancestors and so must receive all that the relatives want to give the dead, including gifts of grain, gold, clothes, even mattresses and slippers. These texts also lay down lists of people who should and should not be invited. Temple priests are not to be invited, indicating that, at this period, there were tensions between Brahmins who followed the Vedic rituals and those who embraced the worship of images in temples that was popular with the masses. These temple priests are clubbed with doctors and moneylenders who are not invited to eat at the shradh. In later times, this would change, with Brahmins who performed funeral rituals being seen as lower in the purity hierarchy as compared to temple priests. Remarkably, Dharma-shastra literature does not talk of pilgrimages, and so the idea of tirtha-shradh probably emerged only in Puranic times as Hindu practices spread to areas beyond the Gangetic plains.

The food offered to the dead in the Dharma-shastra is not just rice (as is the practice now) and barley (as in Vedic times) but also the meat of various animals. No one talks about this any longer, because since the nineteenth century there has been a concerted effort to equate Hinduism with vegetarianism. Across the Dharma-shastra texts—whether written by Apasthamba, Gautama, Manu, Yajnavalkya or Vishnu—there is agreement that hunger is satiated for a longer time with meat. Besides the standard sesame, barley, rice, beans, water, root, shoot and fruit, the recommended foods include fish, deer, sheep, goat, bird, boar, rabbit, turtle, rhinoceros, crane and even domesticated animals. The Buddhists and Jains condemned the meat offerings. Over time, more and more merchants, and later priests, embraced the practice of vegetarianism, making it an indicator of elite Hinduism.

Old stories were being transformed into written epics such as the Ramayana and the Mahabharata at this time, which explicitly explain that a hermit-householder (grihastha) is different from an ordinary householder (grihapati). The grihapati feeds only himself and his family. The grihastha feeds others.

Ramayana

The Ramayana is the story of prince Ram's adventures in the forest. The events that inspired this epic may have taken place nearly 3,000 years ago, around the time that the Vedic culture spread to the lower Gangetic plains of Kosala (modern Ayodhya) and Videha (modern Bihar). But the epic was written down much later. The texts we have now are about 2,000 years old.

In the epic, Ram's father, Dashratha, dies without a son by his side, a tragedy for someone with four sons. His body is preserved in oil and cremated in the absence of his eldest son, revealing how no one can control one's future.

While in exile in the forest, Ram buries the demon Viradha, but cremates the vulture Jatayu, who dies trying to stop the rakshasa-king Ravana from abducting Ram's wife, Sita. When Sita is finally rescued, and Ravana killed, Ravana too is cremated. Ravana's mother is described as a rakshasa-woman, but his father is a Brahmin man, Vaishrava.

Ram's ancestors die prematurely in the story, burnt to death by an angry ascetic called Kapila, who they wrongfully accused of theft. To enable their rebirth, another of Ram's ancestors, Bhagirath, gets the gods to let the celestial river Ganga flow down on earth. Fearing her fall would break the foundations of earth, Bhagirath also enlists the help of Shiva. Shiva, the god of asceticism, smears his body with the ashes of the dead. He catches Ganga in the locks of his hair. When the ashes of the dead are mixed with the waters of the Ganga, we are told, the dead will be born once again and get another chance to live a human life. This story popularised the idea of casting bones of the dead in water, after cremation, and the idea of 'another chance to live'.

The story of the descent of Ganga from heavens to enable rebirth of the dead was first narrated in the Ramayana

Devdutt Pattanaik

Mahabharata

The Mahabharata is one of the world's longest epics, composed around the same time as the Ramayana and the Dharma-shastra. Here we learn of Swarga, the paradise of the Devas, enjoyed by the ancestors who upheld dharma by regularly performing the ritual of yagna to feed the gods. Their stay in Swarga lasted for as long as the Devas had repaid their debt. Thus, Mahabhisha and Yayati and Indradyumna are cast out after their merits run out.

The Mahabharata introduces us to the Pitr-loka where ancestors hang upside down, fearing and awaiting rebirth. Rishis like Agastya and Jaratkaru who shun marriage are tormented by visions of suffering ancestors until they marry and produce children.

The Mahabharata also speaks of another heaven beyond Swarga, for those who do not wish to be reborn. These were Hindu alternatives to the Buddha-loka and Siddha-loka of the monastic orders. The Mahabharata provides us with a glimpse of gloomy Naraka, where people suffer on account of bad karma.

The Mahabharata is also a treatise on the cost of war and violence. Of widows beating their breasts and unbinding their hair to mourn for dead husbands, of orphans wailing. The dead are burnt in the battlefield itself, along with dead horses and elephants, the fuel for which is provided by the wood from broken chariots. This is to prevent dogs and crows from feeding on the flesh of great warriors. So many had died that it was feared that entire forests would have to be cut down to cremate them all individually.

Later regional folk tales related to the Mahabharata draw attention to certain customs and beliefs around death. Pandu, father of the Pandava brothers, tells his sons to eat his flesh after his death in order to acquire his powers. But Krishna stops the orphans from doing so. Sahadeva alone eats a piece of flesh carried by ants and so acquires the power of foresight. He can see everything that is to happen in the future, but Krishna tells him never to share this information voluntarily, for the future is inevitable and nothing can change it, so it is best kept secret. A similar story is told to explain why doctors and leatherworkers are considered impure and why crows are linked to the dead. Dhanwantari, the first doctor, told humans to eat his flesh to obtain all knowledge related to health and healing. But the gods prevented humans from doing so. The only ones who did it were doctors and Chandalas, which is why they are considered impure and shunned. Ants and crows, which eat flesh, were annoyed that the flesh of the dead was being given to fire and water, and so the Brahmins promised to feed them the pinda instead.

Another folklore based on the Mahabharata relates the story of Arjuna mourning his son Abhimanyu, killed in the fifteenth year of his life. To console him, Krishna takes Arjuna to Swarga, where he finds Abhimanyu alive. But Abhimanyu does not recognise Arjuna. When Arjuna persists in calling him son, Abhimanyu says that he has lived many lives and does not remember any of them. In previous lives, he may well have been father to Arjuna too. There is no point in remembering the past; we must focus on the present. The lesson is that dead children need to be forgotten so that we pay more attention to the living ones.

The Gita is part of the Mahabharata, and many people choose to read passages from the Gita after funerals instead of the Garuda Purana. The Gita reinforces the idea of rebirth, the transitory nature of the flesh and the eternity of the soul. 'At birth, the soul wears the flesh as fresh clothes and discards them at the time of death.'

Puranas

As per the Vamana Purana, King Mahiratha chose to stay in Naraka and comfort the dead, just like Yudhishtira in the Mahabharata

The Puranas were composed between the fifth and the tenth century as Brahmins took Vedic culture beyond the Gangetic plains to the rest of India. They offered local kings services related to kingship and statecraft. To establish royal authority and promote the idea of discipline in society, Puranic stories elaborate the nature of Naraka or hell reserved for rule-breakers.

In the Rig Veda, we learn of Naraka for the first time, a dark bottomless pit for wicked people and murderers. This is repeated in the Atharva Veda. In the Shatapatha Brahmana, composed some 500 years later, Naraka is a

Devdutt Pattanaik

place of suffering and pain. In the Mahabharata, it is a sad place with no trees and rivers, its residents lonely and in pain. Then, another 500 or so years later, in the Dharma-shastras of Manu and Yajnavalkya, we find a list of twenty-one hells. The Vamana Purana, an early Purana dated to 500 CE, also speaks of twenty-one hells. However, the Bhagavata Purana, which is from about 900 CE, mentions twenty-eight hells. By the time of the Padma Purana, in 1200 CE, the number has grown further: seven hells, each with six divisions, further divided into two sections, one for crimes committed voluntarily and another for crimes committed involuntarily, bringing the total to eighty-four (7x6x2). The Agni Purana, dated to 1500 CE, speaks of five hells, each with twenty-eight divisions, bringing the total to 140 (5x28). Thus, we see a rising number of hells to punish those who do not follow the rising number of rules that are designed to make society more orderly.

Puranic lore is not just about death and rebirth of human life but also the death and rebirth of the world. The four-yuga concept is amplified upon in it. We learn of pralaya and the death of the world, and how each cosmic rebirth sees the rebirth of a new Manu, a new Vyasa and a set of new seven sages, the Sapta-rishi, who bring back the ancient Vedic ways. This was perhaps in response to the violence that societies experienced and was a way of giving people hope.

In the Puranas, the story of Shiva and Vishnu become prominent. Both gods speak of death, rebirth and liberation. Shiva is linked to the preta and the Chandala in his Bhairava form. We encounter rebirth when Sati reappears as Parvati and marries Shiva. Ram and Krishna, avatars of Vishnu, experience birth and death. Debts incurred in the Ramayana are repaid in the Mahabharata. For example, Ram refuses to look at other women but when he is Krishna he dances with many women. Ram who protects Surya's son Sugriva against Indra's son Vali in Ramayana ends up defending Indra's son Arjuna against Surya's son Karna in the Mahabharata. Thus, the idea of karma was explained through the two epics which captured two lifetimes of Vishnu.

Vishnu is connected to violent deaths through the stories of Parashuram, Ram and Krishna. Parashurama killed the king who killed his father and stole his father's cow. He proceeded to exterminate the line of kings who disrespected dharma. He did pinda-daan for his father with their flesh and offered tarpan with their blood. Later, he forgave the warrior clans and enabled them to repopulate themselves with the help of one warrior who was protected by the Goddess.

The Garuda Purana, a relatively late composition, provides not only an elaboration of hells but also an account of the journey of the dead. This suggests influence of Tantric ideas and shares much with the *Tibetan Book of the Dead*. Here Vishnu educates Garuda who transmits the knowledge to earthly sages who hear the Puranas in the Naimisha forest.

The idea of higher heavens linked to Brahma, Vishnu and Shiva is introduced in the Puranas and later elaborated in Bhakti literature.

Sthala Purana

While the Dharma-shastra literature does not refer to temples and pilgrimages in the context of funeral rites, essays (nibandha) on Dharma-shastra written after the twelfth century make a connection between them. The Puranic literature talks of pilgrimages at length, and encourages everyone to do shradh in these spots to make the ancestors happy. In the Matsya Purana, there are 1,200 verses devoted to pilgrimages, over 3,000 in the Varaha Purana, over 4,000 in the Padma Purana and over 6,000 in the Brahma Purana. In the Skanda Purana, one is told that Aryavarta has over three-and-a-half crore holy pilgrim sites. The contrast between Dharma-shastra and Puranic literature is remarkable indeed.

Pilgrim spots are always located next to vast water bodies, like rivers (Srirangam islands of Kaveri) or even the sea (Ganga Sagar, Rameshwaram). The belief that rivers enable rebirth may have led to the popularity of riverside pilgrim spots such as Godavari's Nashik and Kaveri's Srirangapatanam. Instead of burying bones and ashes as in Vedic times, they were immersed in water. Another ritual that became popular in later times was the ten-day ritual to provide a temporary body to the preta in order to travel to Yama-loka.

Various local Sthala-Purana and Desha-Mahatmya describe where Ram performed shradh for his father. Pilgrims are encouraged to do the same. Spots that bend and turn towards their source are especially sacred. For instance, in Nashik, Ram wanted to perform the shradh ritual at the point where the east-flowing Godavari, that originates nearby, bends and flows westward for a short distance. Similarly, in Kashi, where the south-flowing Ganga turns north briefly. Here, Ravana took the form of a Brahmin and advised Ram to fetch the rare golden deer as an offering to his illustrious father. Offering meat to the dead was a common practice in ancient India, before more and more upper-caste Hindus began to consider meat and blood as a polluting agent in medieval times. While Ram was away hunting, Ravana abducted Sita.

In Rameshwaram, we are told, Ravana himself agreed to perform the shradh rituals for Ram as he was the only Brahmin around. That is why, when Ram killed Ravana, he had to perform rituals in Rameshwaram to wash away the demerit of Brahma-hatya, the crime of killing a Brahmin.

There is also a story about how Ram wanted to perform the shradh ritual in Gaya. He went to the forest looking for suitable offerings and Brahmins who would accept those offerings. While he was away, to Sita's amazement, the spirit of her father-in-law and the ancestors before him arrived and sought offerings from her. She had nothing to give. But the ancestors said that even if she offers them only a ball of sand with affection, they would be content. After the ancestors had been fed with balls of sand and had departed, Sita went to bathe. Ram arrived with Brahmins, and found Sita nowhere. So, he performed the rituals and fed the Brahmins on his own. When Sita returned, Ram chastised her wife for dereliction of wifely duties. Sita explained what had transpired in his absence, but he refused to believe her. She declared the river and the banyan tree of Gaya were her witnesses. The river did not speak up, and so Sita cursed the river at Gaya to flow underground, as it does to this day. The banyan tree of Gaya testified to Sita's honesty. So, even today, pinda offerings are made to the banyan tree of Gaya. Significantly, the story tells us that it is perfectly fine to offer balls of sand, like Sita did, instead of balls of mashed rice as is tradition.

Many pilgrim spots on riverbanks are identified as locations where Ram fed his ancestors

Agama

Agama texts are linked to temple traditions of Hinduism. These texts are especially popular in South India. Temple rituals were designed to humanise the gods, make them participate in human affairs. The immortal gods, for example, do not perform these rituals as they have no ancestors and no need for children. But when Vishnu descends to earth as an avatar, he experiences life and death, and so is obliged to perform this ritual for his parents. Therefore, in many Vishnu temples, we find the deity performing shradh rituals for his parents.

Just before the winter solstice, during the waning moon, an elaborate shradh is held over three days in the Jagannath temple in Puri, Odisha. Lamps are lit, inviting the presiding deity Jagannath's ancestors to eat—most specifically, his parents through various avatars: Aditi and Kashyapa, parents of the Vamana avatar; Kaushalya and Dashratha, parents of the Ram avatar; Devaki and Vasudeva, Yashoda and Nanda, biological and foster parents of the Krishna avatar; and even Gundicha and Indradyumna, who built the Jagannath temple.

Every year, in the month of Magha (January–February), many temples provide pinda-daan to Bhishma of the Mahabharata. He chose to remain celibate so that his father could remarry. As he had no children of his own, Bhishma is trapped in the land of the dead forever, unable to be reborn, and so depends on others for nourishment. This serves a warning to those who choose to be childless and explains the Hindu obsession with marriage and family. In the epic, Bhishma had the power to choose the time of his death. He chose to die after the winter solstice because he wanted to avoid the ancestors who visit humans in the dark and colder half of the year. He died on the eighth day (ashtami) of the waxing moon (shukla-paksha) in the lunar month of Magha, after the sun enters the zodiac of Capricorn (Makara Sankranti), a few weeks after the winter solstice. So, every year, on this day, mashed rice balls are offered to Bhishma in Vishnu temples. It is said that he chanted the thousand names of Vishnu as he lay dying, and Vishnu assured him that he would be remembered for all eternity and fed by the living even though he died childless. This story and ritual are meant to remind people of the importance of establishing a household before considering renunciation and the monastic life.

Tantra

From the eighth to the fifteenth century, we find the rise of Tantra literature. This was the result of Vedic practices spreading via Puranic stories to the wider Indian population across the subcontinent beyond the Gangetic plains. Here, there were many encounters with local practices that clearly valued the body as much as the mind.

More and more scriptures from this period refer to the body (tanu), its koshas (layers), chakras (nodes) and nadis (channels). There are stories of how it is possible for experts in Tantra to leave their flesh and liberate their ghost to travel and occupy the bodies of others. There are sorcerers in these tales that can enslave the preta and turn them into a vetala to do their bidding. More and more temples show images of Shiva and Shakti in their fierce forms of Bhairava and Chamunda alongside the dogs of the cremation grounds. There are stories of ghosts who haunt the living, ghosts who drive people mad, cause sickness, miscarriage and misfortune. Witchcraft and magical rituals gain prominence, and a greater value is placed on astrology, forecasting, geomancy, spirit-calling and other occult rites. Deities are associated with death. Crematoriums become a place of potent dangerous power. In Tantric texts, the female body, sex and violence are combined with transgressive rituals in crematoriums to conquer the fear of death.

There are references to sorcery in folk retellings of the Ramayana and the Mahabharata. Sorcerers are said to have use for the ash, skulls and bones of the dead. This increases the demand for Vedic rituals, where the corpse is destroyed by burning and breaking the skull, and rituals are performed to drive the preta to pitra-loka, away from the reach of sorcerers. This is the period when Hanuman and Bhairava rise in popularity. They are seen as forms of Shiva, who serve goddesses such as Kali who protect people from malevolent spirits.

A whole set of Vedic rituals is prescribed to make rebirth possible. Failing this, it is said, the dead will wander as ghosts, haunting humans, and vulnerable to shamans, sorcerers and other Tantra experts.

There is much in common between the Garuda Purana and the *Tibetan Book of the Dead (Bardo Thodol)* composed by the Guru Padmasambhava. Both show Tantric influence and both emerged in the Tantric Age. The Buddhist work fixes a period of forty-nine days between death and rebirth. It took forty-nine days of contemplation for Siddharth to become Buddha Three phases are described: the one immediately after death when the ghost is confused, the one thereafter which is full of fearful imagery reminding one of attachments and desires, and finally the phase of rebirth for those unable to break free from samsara. Like the Garuda Purana, the Bardo Thodol is read out around the time of death, to facilitate the journey of the dead.

Bhakti

Vedic scriptures insist that rituals must be performed with shraddha, faith, not mechanistically. But typically, Vedic rituals are more about precision and discipline than about emotion. However, over time, emotion came to dominate and overtake ritual practices in India. In the early phase of the Bhakti movement, emotion was very much linked to temples and temple rituals, as we find in the stories of Alvars and Nayamnars of Tamil Nadu who lived around the seventh century. By the time of the sant-kavi tradition in the sixteenth century, however, emotion expressed through song took centre stage.

Ritual started losing its grip in twelfth-century Karnataka with Basava and the sharana gurus of the Lingayat movement valuing direct connection with the divine. The body was smeared with three parallel horizontal ash marks representing the end of the three worlds, and the three bodies, to liberate the spirit, the atma, represented by a pebble worn around the neck.

Around the fifteenth century, a new kind of emotional and romantic bhakti, based on music, started gaining prominence. Some saw the divine with form (saguna) enshrined in temples; others saw it without form (nirguna), without limits or boundaries. In the Tamil Periya Puranam, we hear of Nayanar saints who pass through fire in order to meet their lord inside the temple. There was also the young

Vishnu coming to the rescue of Gajendra. The concept of saviour recurs in devotional traditions.

Devdutt Pattanaik

poet-saint Dyaneshwara who voluntarily gave up his body after translating the Bhagavad Gita into Marathi. In folk songs, we hear of Garuda coming to earth to take the poet-saint Tukaram directly to Vaikuntha. Rajasthani princess-saint Mirabai, we are told, disappears after entering the sanctum sanctorum of a Krishna temple. Some argue these are tales of violence against new ideas challenging orthodoxies couched in mythic metaphor.

In these movements, bhakti becomes the method by which death can be overcome. The Garuda Purana too speaks of bhakti, but not at the cost of ritual. The ritual feeding of the dead must continue, and God's name chanted alongside. This is when the chanting of Ram's name and of Shiva's name becomes part of funerals.

Chanting God's name is supposed to keep death away. When Ajamila chants 'Narayana-Narayana', he is rescued by Vishnu-duta from the clutches of Yama-duta. When Markandeya chants, 'Om Namah Shivayah', he is rescued by Shiva himself from Yama. In the Bengali Ramayana, we are told Ram cannot kill a Rakshasa saint called Tarani-sen because the latter has tattooed his body with Ram's name. Finally, Ram shoots an arrow into his un-tattooed mouth and promises him a place in Saket, the celestial Ayodhya for devotees of Ram. For those who chant Krishna's name, there is a special heaven called Go-loka, where Krishna plays the flute to bring bliss into the hearts of his steadfast devotees.

Islam

Muslims first came to India as traders in South India in the seventh century, then as raiders from the northwest in the tenth century, and finally as rulers who established themselves in Delhi from the twelfth century. They were confronted with Rajput warriors who chose death over perceived dishonour, and whose wives and widows chose to burn themselves rather than be captured by enemies—a controversial and now illegal practice that was once the object of great veneration. This period saw stones and plaques raised to heroes and satis.

Mazaar of a pir in a dargah. Funeral mounds for holy men were raised in India since Buddhist times.

The Muslims bury their dead, with the head often turned in the direction of Mecca. Burial rituals are meant to be simple so that nothing comes between the dead and God. But the sultans of Delhi, flush with wealth, built grand tombs for warlords (emirs) and holy men (pir). This was a Persian practice, quite unlike the simple desert burials of the Arabs, amongst whom Islam first emerged in the early seventh century. The royal mausoleums of these sultans were surrounded by gardens and fountains to remind people of heaven (Jannat), and were inspired by the grand walled gardens that Persian emperors had built since pre-Islamic times. Dargahs were built around the tombs (mazaar) of pirs, much like the Buddhist chaityas built around stupas.

The pre-Vedic rituals of burying the dead in a seated position, once sidelined and frowned upon, returned to the mainstream, especially in the southern parts of India, amongst rich landowners and peasants. More and more monastic orders (matha) became comfortable with the idea of raising a samadhi for the guru. Earlier, even when such memorials existed, they were kept in seclusion, but now they gradually became pilgrim spots. In Rajasthan, and later amongst the Marathas, pavilions known as 'chhatris' where erected at the site where a king was cremated.

Islam believes in Judgement Day (Qayamat). Muslims speak of Azrael, the angel of death, whose subordinate angels took the souls out of the body, forcibly in case of the reluctant and gently in case of the willing. They speak of record-keepers who keep an account of good deeds as well as bad deeds, and of angels who ask the dead soon after burial if they believe in God and his final prophet. Nineteen angels are described as tormenting the wicked in hell.

These concepts intermingled with the Hindu ideas of multiple hells, Yama, Yama-duta and Chitragupta. The thirteenth-century philosopher Madhava from Karnataka even spoke of souls who were unworthy of rebirth, the Tamo-yogyas, who would never be able to rise out of Naraka. The Turkish and Afghan sultans were influenced by Chinese technology and Persian court culture. They introduced pen (kalam) and paper (kagaz) to India. Record-keeping or bahi-khata became an important Hindu concept. Chitragupta, scribe of Yama, was shown with a pen and inkpot in hand. Haridwar, where the Ganga flows into the plains, became a place where family-tree records were maintained by special priests, known as the Panda, in their long notebooks.

Islamic talk of God's mercy appealed to Hindus who chose emotional bhakti-marga over the intellectual gyan-marga and ritualistic karma-marga. The payment of debt liberated the dead in the old days. Now there was an alternative, the mercy of God.

Christianity

While Christ lived in Israel 2,000 years ago, Christianity became a dominant religion only about 1,700 years ago, when the Roman Empire turned Christian, and religion became a political lever to unify and control the empire. And that is why, in the New Testament of the Bible, we find Jesus speaking of God who is merciful and forgiving, while John speaks of God whose angels go to battle against Satan, led by Jesus, the warrior. In the tenth century,

Christian Tombstone

Christianity clashed with Islam. During these crusades, the idea of God as judge dominated the world from Spain to Sindh. The Mongol invasions of the twelfth century popularised the idea of End of the World, and Judgement Day. This probably led to elaboration of concepts such as Kalki and Pralaya in the Puranas.

In fourteenth-century Italy, Dante wrote *The Divine Comedy*. Many have noticed the similarities between the Garuda Purana and *The Divine Comedy*. Unlike the common hell that is peculiar to Christian mythology, Dante describes different hells for different crimes, as does the Garuda Purana. In the narration, Dante is the pilgrim who is accompanied by three people: the intellectual Virgil, the compassionate Beatrice and the mystic St. Bernard, which resonates with the different Hindu paths to moksha. These similarities make one wonder if he was exposed to Puranic writings—although this is unlikely because the Europeans had not yet discovered the sea route to India. Did these ideas spread to Europe via Arabs, like Indian numerals, boardgames and folk tales? We can only speculate.

However, the Garuda Purana and *The Divine Comedy* are not identical as they come from two very different mythic world views. For

Dante, the inferno is a place of eternal suffering, while in the Garuda Purana, hell is a place of temporary suffering, a place to remind a soul not to repeat past misdeeds in future lives. The Garuda Purana's hells are overseen by Yama who, unlike Dante's God, cannot forgive. Only Vishnu or Shiva, the higher gods, have that power. Dante refers to a purgatory where the dead wait until the Final Judgement, a concept not found in Hindu mythology. The Garuda Purana has hells for those who torture and kill animals, something that Dante's work is not concerned with. He focuses instead on punishing soothsayers, fortune-tellers and astrologers, which is not a concern in Hindu mythology. While most punishments are similar, involving weapons, animals and torture, there are some unique punishments that *The Divine Comedy* conjures up. For example, the fortune-teller will spend eternity with the head twisted around to the back rather than facing the front. The proud are forced to bend by carrying heavy weights on their back. The indecisive have to take decisions as they are chased by bees. Dante is strongly influenced by Greek mythology as revealed by references to the river Styx and the three-headed dog Cereberus. In Dante's world, money is bad and poverty is good, an idea not reflected in the Garuda Purana where Lakshmi, the goddess of wealth, is the consort of Vishnu himself, ushering in auspiciousness wherever she goes.

While there are punishments for self-indulgence (lust, greed, gluttony, anger), violence (oppression, exploitation) and maliciousness (jealousy, pride, theft, perjury), there are no specific punishments for falling short of what Hindu scriptures call 'dharma': the responsibility of

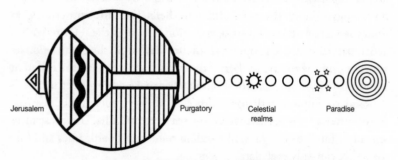

Dante's journey through Hell, Purgatory and Paradise indicates the thirteenth century European understanding of the cosmos when the earth was flat and the sun revolved around it

householders towards the household and of kings towards the kingdom. Dante speaks of hells for those who reject Christianity and for pagans not aware of Christ, a missionary concern not found in Hinduism.

Older forms of Christianity came into India through trade routes nearly 2,000 years ago. However, missionary Christianity came with the Portuguese only in the sixteenth century. With conversion came tensions between the Christian practice of burial and the Hindu practice of cremation. In Goa, there are memories of early converts exhuming the bodies of the dead at night from the church cemetery in order to secretly cremate them in their backyard. This led to the Goa Inquisition to enforce Christian custom and belief on the pagans.

Across India, we find churches with cemeteries full of tombstones with the names and the lifespans of the dead. These became widespread during the British Raj. Christians, like Muslims before them, popularised the idea that a person who dies by suicide should not be buried in sacred consecrated ground. Even today, many ideas related to euthanasia and assisted dying for the old and the sick, and organ donation are influenced by Christian values as the earliest modern hospitals in India were built in British times by Christian missionaries.

Modern Times

The Hindu treatment of widows shocked the Europeans and they wrote about it extensively. This led to the passing of laws forbidding the practice of widow burning and child marriage. Social reformers encouraged the remarriage of widows. While the caste system is frowned upon and forbidden by law, the practice of separate crematoriums for separate castes continues to this day in some places.

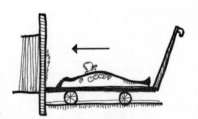

Electric crematorium where the fire pot is placed on the chest of the corpse as symbolic mukha-agni and the breaking of the skull

More and more people are avoiding burning bodies with wood and choose electric crematoriums citing environmental concerns. These days, the feeding of the dead is usually done only on the days immediately after the funeral, during death anniversaries, in the fortnight of the ancestors or during visits to pilgrim spots. Death rituals once performed over several days are now compressed to a single rite.

More and more women perform funeral rituals. They are no longer forbidden in the crematorium. There is increasing talk of allowing informed consent-based assisted death for the old and the infirm, who have completed worldly duties like sages of yore. An increasing number of people are amenable to the idea of donating organs after death, citing the story of Dadhichi's donation of his bones to Indra, and verses from the Vedas that speak of how our flesh reintegrates itself with nature after death: the mind with the moon, the eyes with the sun, the breath with the wind.

Devdutt Pattanaik

Chapter 8

Gods of Death

*In which we appreciate the many
Hindu gods associated with death,
liberation and immortality*

Once, all the gods went to Mount Kailasa to pay their respects to Shiva. Brahma came on his goose, Vishnu on his eagle, Surya on his horse, Chandra on his antelope, Yama on his buffalo. Vishnu's eagle, Garuda, noticed that before entering Kailasa, Yama's eyes fell on a tiny sparrow that had perched itself on a ledge near the gate, chirping a welcome song for all the gods. Yama frowned and crinkled his brow before shrugging his shoulders and joining the gods. Garuda, who was the king of all birds, concluded that the days of the sparrow were numbered. Why else would the god of death frown on seeing it? Perhaps the sparrow would die of starvation on the icy cold slopes of Kailasa. Garuda looked at the little bird—so young, innocent, eager to see the world. Overwhelmed with parental affection, he made a decision: to keep the little sparrow out of Yama's heartless reach. Taking the bird in the palm of his hands, he flew across seven hills and seven rivers until he reached a forest, where he left the bird on a tree laden with tasty fruit. When he returned, he saw Yama smiling at him. Upon his enquiring, Yama revealed, 'When I was entering Kailasa, I saw this sparrow here that was destined to die today, eaten by a python that lives on the mango tree that grows in a forest far away, beyond seven hills and seven rivers. I wondered how he was going to fly there. But you made it happen.' Garuda was horrified. Instead of saving the bird, he had ended up killing it. Then Vishnu said to him, 'You saved the python from starving to death. Is that not a good thing?'

This folk tale draws attention to the inevitability of death. Death exists for life. To live we need food, and for food, predators kill their prey, cattle uproot plants. Basically, when we eat, something dies, directly or indirectly. The deer dies to feed the tiger. Standing trees are consumed by termites. Hundreds of animals and plants are killed to make space for farms that produce food for humans. Thus, life and death are intimately connected. All food is flesh, obtained by killing the living. Life feeds on life (jivo jivatsya jivanam). He who is immortal feeds no one. He who is outside the cycle of birth and death neither eats nor is eaten, neither feeds nor is fed.

If Yama is the god associated with death, then Brahma is the god who creates the cycle of life and death, Vishnu is the god who helps humans cope with the horrors of life and death, and Shiva is the god who breaks the cycle of life and death.

Yama is the oldest god associated with death, mentioned in the Rig Veda. Many other gods linked to different aspects of death have emerged since then. In Vedic times, death rituals were intimately linked with fire, the earth. Niritti was the goddess of decay, degeneration and ghosts, who probably later transformed into the gaunt and ghost-riding Chamunda. Mahabharata personified death as a goddess called Mrityu, who weeps at the thought of having to kill the living. In the Puranas, Shiva roams in the crematoriums, Durga kills the buffalo-demon that is probably representative of Yama, and Vishnu descends on earth as an avatar that experiences birth and death, and so empathises with the human condition. The river-goddess Ganga is intimately linked with rebirth. In the Tantric Age, as more and more people spoke of ghosts and hauntings, the mighty Hanuman became a god to be invoked for protection.

Yama

In the Rig Veda, Yama is the first man to die. He refuses to have sex with his twin sister, Yami, since incest is taboo, and eventually dies childless, to be trapped forever in the land of the dead. He becomes the oldest ancestor, king of the dead. But he also becomes the first sunset and his sister becomes the first night. Another word for night, therefore, is Yamini.

In Zoroastrian mythology that has a common ancestry with Vedic mythology, we hear of Yima, the first human, who protects all animals from a terrible blizzard. Yima is like Manu, who saves all life by gathering plants and animals and placing them on a boat during a great flood, a story we learn from a later text, Shatapatha Brahmana. Yima's name reminds us of Yama while his role is similar to Manu. In Vedic mythology, Yama and Manu are brothers, sons of the sun-god Surya. Yima too is linked with a solar deity. Yama rules the dead; Manu rules the living.

Yama, the ruler of the dead, the model king who has no favourites

Manu's sons establish the solar and the lunar dynasty of kings. Kings are told to emulate Yama because death treats all equally, favouring neither saint nor sinner. Yama, over time, becomes the overseer of the process of rebirth. He ensures that everyone repays their debts. He is fair and dispassionate, without any favourites. He is also wise, explaining to Nachiketa in the Katha Upanishad what happens after death, a role performed by Vishnu in the Garuda Purana.

Yama is visualised as holding a noose in one hand and a staff in another. He travels on a buffalo. The noose is to pull the preta out of the body and the staff is to ensure that no one escapes without repaying their debt. It is well known that no one escapes Yama. The reason why the buffalo is linked to Yama in Puranic literature is not clear. Some speculate that life is bright day, like white sesame and white cows, while death is dark night, like black sesame, and black buffalo. Others say it may be because some buffaloes are difficult to tame, and generally stubborn in nature, like death, which is relentless.

Chitragupta, the scribe who records karma, is the patron deity of the Kayastha community

In the bhakti tradition, Shiva overpowers Yama and becomes known as Yamantaka, one who has overpowered death. Devotees sing a hymn to Shiva, known as Mrityunjaya, that enables the conquest of death. Markandeya, rescued from Yama by Shiva, is the eternal sage who witnesses the creation and destruction of the world and records the passage of time from the pralaya (death of cosmos), all through the four yugas (eras) that constitute a kalpa (life of a cosmos) in the Puranas.

Yama is located in the south, with Agni located to his east and Niritti located to his west. His companion is Chitragupta, the scribe, who holds a book, a stylus and an inkpot in his hand. Yama is also linked to Shani, or the god of Saturn, who in turn is linked with time, or Kala, the one who cuts the week and thus ends time. Shani rides a crow or a vulture, both of which are linked to death. In popular traditions, Yama and Shani are linked to Shiva through Kaal-Bhairava, the god of time who devours everything.

Yama is also linked with dogs, the Sarameya, children of Sarama, the divine female dog who serves Indra. Yama's dogs have four eyes each. In most cultures around the world, death has been linked with dogs. In Greek mythology, there is the three-headed Cereberus. In Egypt, there is the dog-headed Anubis. Dogs with discoloured patches above their eyes are considered to have 'four-eyes' and so are believed to be auspicious and integral to Zoroastrian funeral ceremonies. This is yet another reminder that Zoroastrianism and Hinduism have common roots, though Zoroastrianism, that once flourished in Persia (Iran), is anchored on the idea of one life while Hinduism embraced the idea of rebirth.

Agni

Two-headed Agni, who burns the auspicious and the inauspicious

Balancing the flesh-devouring Agni is Vayu, the wind-god, located in the northwest direction. Vayu is god of wind and god of breath, prana. He enlivens the flesh.

Of the over 1,000 hymns in the Rig Veda, over 200 are dedicated to Agni, the fire-god, through whom the Vedic people connected with the Devas, who lived in the celestial regions.

Agni is called Kravyada when his flames consume a dead body and light the path for preta to travel to the land of the dead. He is called Jataveda when he carries food to the realm of the gods. The two fires are also differentiated. One is the pure fire of the sacrificial altar and is located in the east. The other is the impure fire of the funeral ritual and is lit in the south. Fire itself is visualised as having two faces, one facing east and the other facing south. In Vaastu, Agni is located in the southeast, that is, between the eastern direction of the Devas and the southern direction of the preta.

Agni rides a goat, which was in Vedic times sacrificed to please both the gods and the ancestors. Now no one remembers these ancient practices.

Mrityu

In the Mahabharata, the earth wept as she was crushed by the weight of creatures that never died. To ease her burden, Brahma created Mrityu, the goddess of death. But she refused to do her duty at first and was only persuaded to do so on the condition that she would not have to kill anyone. People would die because of their own karma. She would only enable the process.

This belief that humans die because of their karma, and not because of the will of the gods, is very different from the ancient Greek belief that human lifespans are determined by the length of a thread spun by the fates. The idea of life and death being dependent not on a divine cause but on the consequences of our own actions is reinforced in the Mahabharata when Bhishma tells the Pandavas the story of Gautami, a widow who would not let the fowler Arjunaka hurt the snake whose bite had killed her only child. She said, 'Hurting that snake will not bring back my son. It will only generate demerit that will contribute to our misfortune. My son was killed by his own karma, not because of a serpent.'

Because he created death, Brahma is not worshipped in the way other gods are. Shiva and Vishnu, on the other hand, are worshipped because they enable rebirth and provide the path to liberation.

Niritti

Niritti is the goddess of ghosts and lives in the southwest. She causes rotting and decay. In Vedic literature, she is mentioned as being fearsome and is asked to stay away, for she brings both fear and misfortune. She is linked with Kotravai of Tamil Sangam literature, the wild goddess of the battlefields who eats the flesh of the fallen. She is also linked to Alakshmi, the goddess of misfortune.

If 'degenerative' Niritti sits in the southwest and embodies death and decay, she is balanced by the 'regenerative' moon-crested Ishana-Shiva, who sits in the northeast and embodies the principle of regeneration. This connection with Shiva may be the reason why she is often linked to Chamunda in Tantric and Shaiva lore.

Chamunda

In art, especially from the tenth century CE, when Tantra was on the rise, Chamunda was portrayed as a gaunt goddess, without skin, just a mass of blood-oozing flesh, a skeletal (kankala) form with protruding eyes and fangs, picking her teeth after a meal of flesh. Her companions are wolves, dogs, vultures, crows and maggots. She rides on the back of a preta. She is shown seated on a throne made of corpses.

One of the earliest temples in India is the Vetala Deula, or the temple of the spirit, in Odisha. It is dedicated to Shiva and Shakti in their fiercest forms as Bhairava and Chamunda. Bhairava is shown as having a decaying body, devoid of skin, with fangs and protruding eyes, holding a sword in one hand and a human head in the other. Chamunda is similarly gaunt and fierce, with flames for hair and her body adorned with entrails and limbs of the dead, picking bones and flesh stuck in her teeth. She drinks blood and feasts on the dead. Her companions are the preta, as well as dogs, foxes, crows, scorpions and vultures that feed on dead bodies scattered in a battleground or in a village struck by a terrible epidemic or drought. These temples rose around the same time that stories of Vikramaditya and vetala were being told in royal courts. It was during this period of history that death and afterlife became an integral part of Tantra-linked sorcery and Indian folklore.

In Puranic lore, Bhairava is called Bhuta-pati, the master of ghosts, and he rides a dog. These ghosts of Bhairava are different from the dead of Yama-loka, who await rebirth. They have not crossed Vaitarni and are trapped in the land of the living because their relatives have not performed the Vedic rites of the dead. Daksha, the primal Vedic priest, son of Brahma, does not like Shiva and shuns him. He considers Shiva impure. But Daksha's daughter, Sati, defies her father and marries Shiva. An angry Daksha performs a yagna to which he refuses to invite his daughter and her husband. He has food served to everyone who is present, except Sati and Shiva. Angry at this insult, Sati jumps into the yagna fire, offering her body as food to Shiva. Daksha remains indifferent to her death and proceeds with the ceremony, angering Shiva, who transforms into Bhairava and beheads him. But the Devas beg Shiva to curtail his anger and forgive Daksha and restore him back to life.

This dramatic story comes from the post-Vedic Puranas. It is not found in the Vedas, Vedangas or Vedanta. Here, Shiva is linked to death, ghosts and impurity, while Daksha is linked to life, immortality and purity. The two worlds are brought together by the goddess, Daksha's daughter Sati, who in Shiva's company becomes the corpse-eating, fearsome Chamunda. She is making sure that the Vedic world of ritual purity learns from Shiva, who speaks of rebirth and immortality. This clash of two ideas may have inspired the belief that even leftover food (ucchista) is an offering. Consumed by dogs and crows, it is an offering to the god of wandering ghosts, who takes care of those left behind on this side of the Vaitarni.

Chamunda, who picks her teeth after eating decaying flesh, sits on corpses and rides a ghost. She is probably a later manifestation of Niritti, the goddess of decay and the guardian of the southwest direction.

Shiva

Harappa has seals showing a man seated in yogic posture that may indicate a kind of proto-Shiva. The Vedas refers to Rudra, a feared wild deity, linked with animals and plants. By the time the Puranas were composed, Shiva was a popular manifestation of the divine, a hermit who becomes a householder. This narrative rose as a counter to Buddhism, the new religion that was challenging the old Vedic ways and promoted giving up household life in favour of monasticism.

He was imagined as emerging from a pillar of fire that had no beginning and no end. In other words, he was neither born nor did he die. He was self-created: swayambhu. His children, Ganesha and Kartikeya, were ayonija, not born of the womb. Thus, they were outside the wheel of rebirths.

Shiva wanders in the crematorium like a Chandala, smearing his body with ash, holding in his hand the skull of Brahma, reminding all of death. In his Bhairava form, he rides a dog, a symbol of the cremation ground. He is surrounded by preta, the ghosts of the dead. From his hair flows the Ganga, offering the promise of rebirth.

Shiva does not see the point of marriage, children, kitchen or household, as he is immortal and has no ancestors to feed. He owes no one anything as he is the supreme hermit and has no property or attachments, or karmic burden. But the goddess tells him, 'Those who are not hungry must produce food for the hungry. Have compassion for those who experience birth and death, even if you have conquered birth and death.' So, Shiva descends from Mount Kailasa, the abode of the immortals, and goes to Kashi, on the banks of the Ganga, where he lives as a householder amongst those who experience birth and death.

Mukha-linga (mask) of Shiva-linga with three eyes, a trident, three-leafed bilva sprig, and three parallel horizontal lines referring to the three-fold nature of time, space, matter and body

Since Shiva sits in the north, facing the south, he is called Dakshina-murti. His wife is called Dakshinayani, daughter of the chief Brahmin, Daksha, who comes from the south (dakshina). She is called

Dashina Kali or Smashan Kali, and is shown as dark, ferocious and naked, bedecked with the heads and limbs of the dead, her tongue sticking out, her hair unbound. She is the patron of Tantric teachers, who disregard rules of impurity and believe that wisdom lies beyond Brahminical notions of purity. If Shiva is the north, Shakti is the south. If Shiva is the soul, Shakti is the flesh. If Shiva rejects sex and violence, she embodies sex and violence. He is Purusha and she is Prakriti. Together, they create the world. She turns the hermit into the householder. He turns the wild forest into the regulated garden. In this process emerges the divide between the pure and the impure: forbidden, untamed forests and welcoming, controlled fields. Those who know that such boundaries and divisions are man-made rise above hierarchies and become the wise ones.

In art, fire and ash represent defeating death with immortality, while water represents defeating death through regeneration. Both are linked to Shiva, who smears his forehead with three horizontal lines of ash collected from funeral pyres, indicating the death of three worlds and three bodies, and release of atma. From his head flows the Ganga, in which the bones of the dead are immersed to enable rebirth. If Shiva is swayambhu, his consort, Shakti, is the womb or yoni through which the dead return to the world of the living. Their children are ayonija, born by bypassing the womb.

Fire is physical fire that needs fuel. But tapa is spiritual fire that does not need fuel. It is churned in the mind through ascetic practices known as tapasya, which involves control of breath, body and mind. The point of tapasya is not to gain power but to outgrow the need for power, through wisdom. So, Shiva, the supreme tapasvin, sits in the north, facing south, the direction of death, teaching people how to conquer death through sense control and to overcome memories and desires. Shiva releases the fire of tapa from his third eye to kill desire (kama), which is why he is called Kamantaka. He also destroys memory (smara), which is why he is called Smarantaka. In Shiva lore, the point of tapa is to rise above the cycle of life and death. The three horizontal lines of ash (tripundra) that Shiva marks his forehead with is the end of the three worlds and the three bodies that we occupy. That is why he is called destroyer of three worlds (Tripurantaka). Unfortunately, most people who churn tapa seek power over the world, rather than escape from the world. They seek siddhi rather than samadhi.

Shakti

When Sati dies by jumping into the pit of Daksha's sacred fire, Shiva takes her charred corpse and wanders the earth. Seeing that he is trapped in memory and sorrow, the Devas ask Vishnu to liberate him. Vishnu hurls his discus and cuts Sati's corpse into tiny pieces, which fall in different parts of India and become the sites of major power. At each of these Shakti-peeth, or the seats of the goddess, is located a temple dedicated to the goddess. Jwalamukhi, in the north, is where her tongue falls. Kamakhya, in the east, is where her womb falls. There are other temples where her eye, hands, feet, breasts have fallen. Even in death, the goddess transmits her power, reminding all that, in nature, life and death are natural processes that follow each other.

In the first story of rebirth ever told in the Puranas, Sati returns as Parvati, the princess of the hills, and marries Shiva once again. Only, this time, she approaches Shiva not after defying her father but through love and devotion. She does not choose her husband over her father; she unites them. She gets Shiva to become a groom and come to her father's house, and participate in Vedic marriage rituals. She makes him set up a home and father children, howsoever reluctantly. Thus, she turns the hermit into a householder and a father of two sons, Ganesha and Kartikeya.

But Shiva and his children are immortals. They have no ancestors to feed. So, Parvati makes Shiva descend from the icy mountains of Kailasa to the vibrant city of Kashi on the banks of the Ganga. In Kailasa, a mountain of stone covered with snow, there is no vegetation. But then, Shiva needs no food. In Kashi, Parvati becomes Annapoorna and cooks food. She draws Shiva's attention to the cries of the preta, the ghosts in the many crematoriums on the banks of the Ganga. She asks him to feed them. So, Shiva becomes a beggar, Bhikshatan, who begs Parvati for food and feeds the dead in his compassion. He also becomes a guard, the Kotwal who protects

Shiva is smeared with ash from crematoriums, a reminder of death, but by making him husband and father, Shakti draws attention to rebirth

Devdutt Pattanaik

the city from ghosts. In the city of Kashi, Shiva is worshipped as Kaal-Bhairava, who rides a dog and reminds everyone of death that awaits the living, in the hope that they will focus on the means to break free from the wheel of rebirths.

Shiva's transformation from hermit to householder is about compassion for the dead, to be experienced even by those who are immortal. Sati and Parvati remind Shiva that while he is Maha-Deva, one who has outgrown hunger, the ordinary gods, the Devas, are hungry for food. She draws attention to the idea of hunger which sustains culture, and counters the monastic narrative of fasting and withdrawing from the sensory and material world. Thus, through the story of Shiva, we see the Brahmin order challenging the Buddhist and Jain doctrines that favour hermits over householders.

Ganga

Ganga, the river-goddess, is linked with rebirth. Her story is first told in the Ramayana: how she once flowed in the paradise of the gods, how she was made to descend on earth, and how her fall would have broken earth's foundations had Shiva not caught her in the locks of his matted hair. This is a metaphor for the destructive power of material life, represented by the river, and the protective power of yoga and tapasya, embodied in Shiva, the hermit. Ganga then is the archetypal water-nymph (apsara). Those whose ashes and bones are immersed in Ganga escape life as a ghost and get a chance to be either reborn or liberated.

In the Mahabharata, Ganga is the wife of Shantanu. She drowns her newborn babies who are actually the celestial Vasu, cursed to experience mortality. But humans see her action as infanticide and so she leaves the human realm.

She is visualised riding a makara, an elephant-headed fish, which is probably a river-dolphin. She holds a pot, symbol of the womb. Her movement is seen as serpent-like, linking her to the Nagas.

Ganga, the river-goddess who enables rebirth. She flows on earth through the matted locks of Shiva's hair.

If Gauri (Parvati) sits on Shiva's lap, then Ganga sits on his head. Both engage the hermit with the householder's life.

Kali

The Tantric Age saw the emergence of many goddesses who were associated with death, cremation grounds, ghosts and sorcery. We learn of goddesses who were linked to miscarriages and childhood fevers. We hear of groups of women who lived in forests and waters and were feared and revered, such as Matrikas and Mahavidyas. Amongst them were Tara and Kali, who were visualised as dancing on corpses, adorned with the heads and limbs of fallen warriors. We find descriptions of goddesses like Chinnamastika, who stand atop corpses and copulating couples, cut off their own head and drink their own blood, thus displaying full mastery over the forces of life and death, hunger and fear.

These goddesses are invoked by sorcerers seeking Siddha powers that would enable them to conquer death, change shape and size, manipulate minds, fly in the air, walk on water, and leave their body to travel through astral planes and communicate with ghosts. In Adbhuta Ramayana, influenced by Tantric ideas, Mahiravana seeks to sacrifice Ram and Lakshman to Kali in Patala, but Hanuman beheads Mahiravana instead and makes Kali sensitive to human fear of death and ghosts.

Chinnamastika is differentiated from Kali. Kali sticks out her tongue to drink the blood of the Asura who wishes to regenerate. Thus, she blocks regeneration—and stops the wheel of rebirths. Kali is differentiated from

Chamunda, who has a gaunt skeletal form, feeds on flesh and death and is not linked to regeneration or liberation. But more often than not, Chamunda, who sits on a pile of corpses, is conflated with the self-beheading Chinnamastika, and with Kali or Tara, who dance atop Shiva and unite with him. This sexual union of the Tantric Shiva and Shakti is a visual manifestation of the abstract Vedic concept of Purusha and Prakriti.

Kali stepping on Shiva. Without her Shiva is shava (corpse).

Devdutt Pattanaik

Durga

Durga is the goddess of kings and of war and is shown battling and defeating a demon who has taken the form of a buffalo, which is the mount of Yama, the god of death. As Mahishasuramardini, killer of the buffalo-demon, she is not just battling the enemy; she is battling death itself.

This is implied by the fact that Durga is worshipped in the ten days that follow the fortnight of the ancestors. The first day of prayer is called Mahalaya, the great dissolution, a reminder of how she enables the shift from death to new life. In this time, she is also called Shakambari, the goddess of vegetation, and her worship coincides with the harvest before as well as after the rains. Her warrior aspect is linked to the sickle and plough. Her maternal aspect is visualised as a pot full of germinating grains and a sheaf of medicinal herbs and creepers.

Durga killing the buffalo-demon. The buffalo is symbolic of Yama and so death.

All this makes Durga, the warrior goddess, also the mother goddess, one linked with death, even liberation, and the other linked with rebirth.

In some folk traditions, the buffalo is worshipped as a god, the temporary husband of Durga, whose death enables rebirth. Hence, buffaloes are sacrificed during Durga festivals and their blood is mixed with seeds. This idea of death and regeneration linked to fertility is an ancient theme associated with agricultural communities around the world. The earth is the goddess. Metaphorically, the harvest denotes the killing of the old husband and the birth of a new one, who will sow the next season's seed.

It is known that the buffalo was tamed in the Harappan cities (2600–1900 BCE) and exported to Mesopotamia. It may have been a symbol of death since ancient times. Harappan cities also have images of goddesses who are half-tigers, like the Sphinx. This suggests some continuity with modern worship of the tiger-riding mother-goddess (Sheravali).

The earliest image of a goddess battling and overpowering a buffalo dates back to the Kushana period in 100 CE. This image is the earliest depiction of the goddess who, by the seventh century, came to be known as Mahishasuramardini and was identified with Durga, the fierce wife of Shiva. By this time, she was linked to royalty. Warriors who lead battles and kill their enemies to become kings invoke Durga's power in order to conquer their fear of death. Ram invokes her in the Ramayana. The Pandavas invoke her in the Mahabharata. They offer the heads of their enemies to Durga, who rewards them with dominion.

Vishnu

The stories about Vishnu complement the stories about Shiva. Shiva is immortal, so he does not feed the dead. His children are born without passing through a womb, and so do not experience birth or death. By contrast, Vishnu enters the mortal world through the womb. As an avatar, he has parents and children who die, and for whom he performs funeral rituals. Vaman performs the rituals for Aditi and Kashyapa, and Parashuram for Renuka and Jamadagni. Ram performs the rituals for Kaushalya and Dashratha, and Krishna for Devaki and Vasudev, as well as for his foster parents, Yashoda and Nanda. We find pilgrim spots where these rituals are said to have been performed by Ram: Kurukshetra, Pushkar, Puri, Nashik, Gaya, Rameshwaram. Ram even asks Hanuman to serve the living by protecting them from the dead, which is why Hanuman is evoked when people fear being haunted and possessed by ghosts.

We are told that Vishnu takes the form of Parashuram, Ram and Krishna to kill wicked kings in order to lessen the burden of earth. Thus, Vishnu is also the instrument of death. Death and time exist to ensure dharma on earth. As Ram, Vishnu voluntarily ends his life by entering the river Sarayu after completing his worldly duties. As Krishna, Vishnu goes to the land of the dead and brings back to the world of the living the ghost of his

Krishna presenting the
Bhagavad Gita to Arjuna

Devdutt Pattanaik

teacher Sandipani's son, who was killed prematurely. He also brings back the ghosts of his six elder brothers, who were killed at birth by Kansa. These ghosts meet their parents on earth and return to Yama-loka. As Krishna, Vishnu reveals the secret of rebirth and liberation to Arjuna, a discourse he later gives to Uddhava before his death. The death of Vishnu's avatars is not really death, as Vishnu simply gives up his mortal form and returns to Vaikuntha rather than go to Yama-loka. Such stories reinforce how the wisdom of the Vedas, that is, atma and yoga, revealed in texts like the Bhagavad Gita and the Uddhava Gita, enables one to bypass the wheel of rebirths.

In Shiva's heaven, Kailasa, no one is hungry. But Vishnu knows the importance of hunger in provoking compassion and reflection. So, Vishnu's heaven Vaikuntha is the ocean of milk, where there is food for all who are willing to share. This is why Shiva is called the destroyer while Vishnu is called the preserver. Hindu mythology makes sense when we appreciate the centrality of hunger in Hindu metaphysics.

Hanuman

The story of the mighty Hanuman comes from the epic Ramayana, where he helps Ram rescue his wife Sita, who has been abducted by the rakshasa-king Ravana. He is linked with restraint, celibacy, contentment and service. He is both strong and wise, master of the Mantra (from manas, meaning mind) and the Tantra (from tanu, meaning body). Visualised as a monkey, he is more powerful than a human. That his father is Vayu, lord of wind and breath, connects him with yoga. That his teacher is Surya, the sun, connects him with the Vedas.

As the Ramayana became popular, Hanuman began to be seen as a form of Shiva, who protects humans in times of difficulty. As fear of the occult and ghosts peaked in the Tantric Age between the eighth and the fifteenth centuries, Hanuman became popular as a protector against ghosts, as well as sorcerers who enslaved ghosts. Thus,

Pancha-mukhi Hanuman

in the Sanskrit Adbhuta Ramayana, from the fifteenth century, we learn of Patali Hanuman, who goes to the subterranean regions where everything is upside down. There, he overpowers Mahiravana and his son, Ahiravana, the sorcerers who wish to offer the head of Ram to Kali, in order to obtain magical Siddha powers. He rises back to earth transformed, having sprouted four more heads: that of a lion, an eagle, a horse and a boar. In other words, the goddess grants him powers over all occult forces to defeat all malevolent and degenerative forces. Hanuman is often shown facing south, just like Shiva's Dakshinamurti form. He keeps death and ghosts at bay.

In folk Ramayanas it is said that Yama fears Hanuman so much that he refused to enter Ayodhya, the city of Ram. The gods tell Ram that his period on earth is over and he needs to return to Vaikuntha. For that Ram has to die, but he cannot die as long as Yama does not enter Ayodhya, and this will not happen as long as Hanuman guards the gates of the city. To distract Hanuman, Ram drops his ring and it slips into a crack on the floor. Ram asks Hanuman to fetch it. The crack in the floor is a tunnel that leads Hanuman to Patala. There he finds a mountain made of duplicates of Ram's rings. Vasuki, king of the Nagas, explains the mystery to Hanuman, 'Our world goes through death and rebirth. In each lifespan, the world witnesses the arrival of Ram. Then Ram's ring falls to Patala, a monkey follows it, and Ram on earth dies, shedding his mortal coil to return to Vaikuntha. As many rings in the mountain, so many Rams have come and gone. Hanuman has met each one of them, for he is immortal, but he forgets, and tries to save them all, in vain.'

Devdutt Pattanaik

Outsmarting Death

*In which we learn how ideas of immortality and
regeneration manifested through tales of
Soma, Amrita, Sanjivani and Chiranjeevi*

Kshaya means decay and degeneration, a natural process. Akshaya means never-withering, which is a mythic imagination. This can be of four types. The first involves avoiding degeneration entirely by being immortal, which gives rise to the concepts of Amrita and Chiranjeevi. The second is about regeneration, renewal, constantly restoring health and youth, and delaying death, which gives rise to ideas such as Sanjivani, Naga-mani, Pati-vrata and Rasayana. The third is having faith that all things that die come back to life eventually. This is wisdom, that grants liberation (moksha) from death, and ends fear of death. The fourth type is having faith in a divine being that never experiences birth or death, who bypasses the womb (ayonija) or is self-created (swayambhu).

Soma

In Vedic times, Soma juice, squeezed out of the Ephedra shrub, was offered to the gods on the occasion of the full moon and the new moon, drawing attention to its waxing and waning. Ephedra contains chemical stimulants that make one alert and active. But in Puranic times, Soma was linked with the moon, and its ability to regenerate. The moon, in turn, was connected to Shiva and Ganga.

113

Shiva placing the moon on his head to help it regenerate

In the Soma-nath Sthala Purana, the moon god is cursed with the disease of degeneration. Each day, he loses a bit of his lustre. To save himself from oblivion, he worships Shiva, the god linked with death and rebirth, from whose topknot flows the river of heaven, Ganga. Shiva places the moon on his forehead, giving him access to the magical Soma, which restores his lustre. And so, the waxing and waning moon is linked to regeneration and rebirth, and is renamed Soma, the very substance that rescued him.

Monday, that is, Soma-vaar, the day of the moon god, is linked to rebirth and regeneration. In popular culture, when the new-moon night falls on a Monday, millions make their way to the Ganga to bathe in it, hoping to liberate their ancestors and their children from the curse of death and bless them with the boon of regeneration. This day is called Somavati Amavasya or Sompati Masya.

Amrita

The Rig Veda speaks of a world of permanence where nothing decays. In the Mahabharata, the gods crave immortality (Amrita). Swarga, the paradise of these gods, is called Amravati, the immortal city, where no one grows old or dies. To obtain Amrita, the ocean of milk was churned (manthan) with a giant spindle made of Mount Meru, kept afloat by a giant turtle. Vasuki, the Naga king, served as the churning rope.

In the later Puranic tradition, Vishnu takes centre stage in the story. The ocean of milk is his abode. His eagle, Garuda, carries Mount Meru while he takes the form of a turtle that keeps the churning spindle afloat. The churning rope is not Vasuki but Vishnu's serpent, Adi Ananta Sesha. The Devas from the sky pull the tail end of the rope while the Asuras pull the other end. The aim is to release Shri, goddess of fortune, who has dissolved herself in the ocean. The churning causes the serpent to spew out venom, Halahala, which is digested by Shiva. Then emerge fourteen jewels (ratna), one for each phase of the moon. The list varies across texts. But they can be classified as jewels that bestow authority (dharma), prosperity (artha) and pleasure (kama).

Authority is symbolised by the elephant, horse, umbrella and bow that emerge like butter churned out of milk. Prosperity is symbolised by the wish-fulfilling tree, the wish-fulfilling cow, the wish-fulfilling jewel and the cornucopia that overflows with grain and gold. Pleasure is represented by the gandharvas who make music, the apsaras who dance, the kinnaras who sing, as well as wine and the moon, which contribute to the joyful mood. Then comes Shri, the goddess of fortune, who chooses Vishnu as her husband. With her comes Dhanvantari, the god of health and healing, who carries the pot of Amrita and brings with him the knowledge of Ayurveda.

Both Devas and Asuras want to be immortal. As they fight over the Amrita, Vishnu takes the form of the enchanting damsel Mohini and offers to divide it fairly between them. Everyone agrees to submit to the decision of the beautiful one. Mohini starts pouring the Amrita first in the mouth of the Devas. Seven Devas receive it and become the seven visible planets, the graha. This makes one of the Asuras, Svarbhanu, suspicious and he moves to sit among the Devas. The sun and the moon figure this out and complain to Vishnu, who cuts off the Asura's head as he is about to swallow the nectar. As a result, the Asura is split in two: the immortal head named Rahu, which chases the sun and the moon, causing eclipses, and the immortal body named Ketu, which does not know where to go and travels restlessly across the sky as a comet. Thus, Amrita is linked to the eternal unblinking celestial bodies, the graha, to eclipses and to comets, the nine players of Hindu astrology.

The incident destroys the temporary truce between the Devas and the Asuras. The Devas, rendered immortal by the Amrita, claim all the treasures and rise to the sky. The mortal Asuras sulk under the earth and swear never to let the Devas enjoy their treasures in peace. They will attack Amravati and turn Swarga into a battleground, eternally under siege. The Devas have all the wealth, but since they do not share they have no peace, a warning to rich humans

Devas and Asuras churning the ocean of milk for Amrita, the nectar of immortality

who do not perform the five yagnas meant to feed the hungry, including plants, animals, gods, family and strangers.

We are told that drops of Amrita fell on earth at various spots, where temples rose and festivals are celebrated. Those who visit those temples and participate in those festivals benefit from Amrita. As a result, decay (kshaya) is removed from the life and replaced by relentless growth (akshya) and prosperity (vriddhi).

Sanjivani

Shiva gave a rishi called Shukra access to Sanjivani. Sanjivani is sometimes presented as a herb (Sanjivani-buti) and sometimes as a ritual technique (Sanjivani-vidya) that enables the dead to come back to life. Shukra took this knowledge and gave it to the Asuras to help them in their war against the Devas. Shukra hated the Devas because his mother was beheaded by Vishnu when she tried to protect the Asuras from the Devas. Vishnu was cursed for this crime of killing a woman—he was forced to be born on earth and experience mortality as Ram and as Krishna.

The Asuras, like the Nagas, are residents of Patala, the subterranean regions. If the Nagas are linked to gems, which they sprout on their hoods, the Asuras are linked to metal that springs from their bones. The Asuras are able to replenish the earth constantly. Water sources are renewed, plants bring forth fresh flowers and fruit year after year. What is the secret?

The Asuras would not share. They also misused their powers, as we

Hanuman carrying the mountain with the Sanjivani herb

learn from the story of Atapi and Vatapi, two Asura brothers. Atapi would turn his brother into a goat, kill him and feed him to guests. Vatapi would then regenerate in the guest's belly, tear out his guts and emerge gleefully. This way, the Asura brothers could feed Brahmins and earn spiritual merit without having to give them gifts. Their reign of terror was finally stopped by Agastya, who ate Vatapi, the goat, and digested him before he could renew himself. He then took the wealth of Atapi and walked away chuckling, having avenged all the Brahmins killed before him.

To steal the secret of Sanjivani-vidya from the guru of Asuras, the Devas deploy Kacha, son of their guru Bhrihaspati, who charms Shukra's daughter, Devayani. The Asuras grow suspicious and kill Kacha but Devayani forces her father to revive him. The Asuras then kill Kacha again and this time, they feed Shukra his flesh. Shukra can no longer resurrect Kacha without killing himself. But Devayani begs her father to share his knowledge with his student, so that a resurrected Kacha can then revive Shukra. Kacha is thus saved but since he emerges from Shukra's body, he declares Devayani his sister, breaking her heart, and returns to the realm of Devas.

The most popular reference to Sanjivani comes from the Ramayana. Here, it is a herb that grows atop Mount Gandhamadana, which is carried by Hanuman and brought to Lanka, so that Ram can restore Lakshman, mortally injured in battle, back to life.

Ayurveda

Dhanvantari, the god of health and healing, emerged from the ocean of milk carrying Amrita, the nectar of immortality. The grass on which this pot was kept became immortal, its blades springing back every time they are plucked. This is the kusha/darba grass that is sacred in Vedic and temple rituals. It is tied around the ring finger (Pavitra) for purification during Vedic rituals. It is also offered to Ganesha in temples. Serpents, it is said, have the power to

Amrita was placed on kusha grass which is why this grass is integral to Vedic rites

shed and regenerate skin because they spend all their lives crawling on this immortal grass. It is Dhanvantari who teaches Ayurveda to humans. Thus, we find Amrita, Sanjivani and Ayurveda, all linked through Dhanvantari.

The Mahabharata tells us how the secret of immortality, of Soma, was not shared by the Devas. Indra, the rain god, refuses to give it to the Ashwini twins, sons of Surya, the sun god. Indra tells all the rishis who know the secret not to share it with anyone. They are warned that their

Dadhichi with a horse's head revealing the secret of Soma to the Ashwini twins

head will split into a thousand pieces if they do. But the Ashwini twins have a plan. They replace the head of Rishi Dadhichi with that of a horse. Through the horse head, they learn the secret of Soma. When the horse head explodes, they replace it with Dadichi's original head.

The Ashwini twins then use this knowledge to restore the youth of Rishi Chavanya. Chyavana, in turn, teaches humans Ayurveda, which uses the power of chants, the phases of the moon, various plants, gems and metals to cure disease and delay death. In the Ramayana, when Hanuman is bringing the Sanjivani, he also destroys malevolent spirits like Kalanemi and gains controls over malevolent planets such as Saturn (Shani), a reminder of the ancient belief that healing is not just a function of herbs but also a function of occult and astrology.

Naga-mani

The Nagas have Naga-mani, a jewel that old and wise Nagas sprout on their hoods. This Naga-mani contains the power of healing and can be used to cure diseases and reverse decay. It can even bring the dead back

The serpent-jewel that has the power to heal and revive the dead

to life. In the Mahabharata, when Arjuna is killed by his son, Babruvahana, Arjuna's Naga wife Ulupi brings a Naga-mani to restore him to life.

Astrologers, who are experts in Jyotisha-vidya, believe that gems and metals found under the earth come from the Nagas and the Asuras and contain the power of Sanjivani, just as the celestial bodies in the sky, the graha, contain Amrita. These can be used to remove negative forces from one's life and bring in positive forces. Negative forces cause decay, gloom and death. Positive forces enable growth, joy and longevity.

Tapa

In the Puranic stories, which started being composed from the fifth century onwards, Asuras are shown performing tapasya, churning of tapa or spiritual fire in the body that compels even Brahma and Shiva to give them boons: Brahma, because he is their father; Shiva, because he is a guileless one (Bhole-nath) who does not take sides. The Asuras seek boons to become immortal, but they know these will not be granted as nothing in nature is immortal. So, they seek boons to outsmart death. But each time, the Devas, or Vishnu, take advantage of loopholes to kill the ambitious Asuras. Yet, the Asuras keep coming back, thanks to Sanjivani, never letting the Devas enjoy their pleasures in peace.

Hiranyakashipu says he should not be killed by anything human or animal, at day or at night, inside a dwelling or outside a dwelling, so he is killed by Vishnu in the form of Narasimha, who is neither man nor animal, at twilight, which is neither day nor night, on the threshold, which is neither inside nor outside a dwelling. Taraka asks that he be killed by a baby who can do battle, and so the Devas get Shiva to father a son who is so powerful that he needs multiple wombs to develop in. This son is a fully armed warrior on the sixth day of his life and is able to kill Taraka. Mahisha is killed by the goddess Durga because he wishes that no creature may kill him, but uses only the male pronoun, thus neglecting to ask for protection from women. Ravana is killed by Vishnu, who takes the form of Ram, because he seeks protection from all creatures of the cosmos except humans. Victories of the Devas are constantly followed by the appearance of another Asura. Indra's throne is constantly wobbling and under threat. Nothing lasts forever. Neither power, nor prosperity or pleasure. Neither life nor death.

Narasimha, who is neither animal nor human, killing the Asura Hiranakashipu who tried to outsmart death

The idea of tapasya comes from hermits who withdrew from the world. But later, these hermits were seen as sorcerers with magical ability to defy death and even control the world. Tapasya was seen not merely as a meditative practice but as an esoteric technique to generate tapa or heat within the body that can be used by tapasvis, or fire-ascetics, to gain supernatural abilities, such as walking on water, flying in air, changing shape and size, and even conquering death.

Tapasya demands celibacy, sense-restraint and yoga practices. Their enemies are the apsaras, damsels who can enchant and distract the ascetics. The word 'apsara' is derived from water (apsa) and so is the opposite of fire (tapa). Therefore, the opposition of apsaras and tapasvis seems natural. In Tantra, apsaras are linked with worldly pleasures and death, and so equated with dangerous yoginis and dakinis. In the Tantric Age, from around tenth century CE, the idea arose that loss of semen is the cause of disease, degeneration and death. Those who could reverse the semen flow, make it rise up the spine through occult practices, could regenerate the moon inside the brain (Soma) and attain immortality as well as magical powers.

Rasayana

By the tenth century, Hanuman's superhuman abilities to fly across the sea and change his size and shape at will were being explained as the consequence of his celibacy. We are told that Hanuman's sweat was so powerful that a drop of it could get a fish pregnant. Thus was born Makaradhvaja, half-fish and half-monkey, guardian of Patala, the subterranean realm of sorcery, regeneration and magic.

This is also when we hear legends of the Nath-jogis of North India and the Siddhas of South India, who had magical powers known as Siddhi, including the power to fly in the air, walk on water, change their shape and size, manifest food and other objects at any time or place. Also, they could not be killed. All this because they knew special breathing and meditation practices that reversed the flow of semen up the spine and thus kept mortality at bay. They could sexually exhaust enchanted women known as yoginis without losing a drop of their own sexual fluid. This was said to be the source of their power.

In Nath folklore, Raja Gopichand buries Jalandar-nath alive in a pit of horse manure, but after several years Jalandar-nath emerges alive, revealing his power over death. Gorakh-nath kills Mina-nath by striking him to the ground as a washerman strikes wet clothes against a stone.

He hangs the corpse to dry on a clothesline, and then resurrects him. He does this so many times that Matsyendra-nath, Mina-nath's father and Gorakh-nath's guru, is shaken out of his stupor and remembers once again how the world of life, death, pleasure, prosperity and power is all delusion for those who follow the path of Nath-jogis. By his powers, Revan-nath was able to bring back to life the seven children of a couple who had died young. These celibate ascetics are able to do what, until then, only God could do. Through ritual observance they become God-like on earth: immortal with magical powers.

The Nath-jogis were masters of rasayana, or occult alchemy. They considered mercury to be the semen of Shiva and sulphur to be the menstrual discharge of Shakti. They had a complex understanding of human anatomy and physiology. They spoke of concentric layers of the body (kosha), the vertical nodes of the body (chakra) strung together by channels (nadi), enlivened by breath (prana). This focus on the body that we find in Tantra is very different from the focus on the mind that is found in earlier Upanishadic Buddhist and Jain lore. Here outsmarting death was not an intellectual idea; it was a tangible experience. Some historians believe contacts with China may have contributed to the popularity of this idea.

A Nath-jogi who acquires Siddhi or occult powers through yoga and tapasya

Chiranjeevi

In direct contrast to the idea that death is inevitable and nothing lasts forever, Hinduism also has the concept of Chiranjeevi, the eight immortal ones. This idea was probably influenced by the Chinese idea of eight immortals.

China and India have had a long historical contact by three routes: the land routes across Central Asia, the mountain passes of Bhutan and Burma and the sea routes via Southeast Asia. Chinese monks came to India from around the fifth century CE to translate the original Buddhist scriptures and must have shared Taoist ideas in exchange. In Taoism,

Markandeya witnessing Pralaya, the flood of doom, on which Krishna floats cradled by a fig leaf

immortality is not a spiritual concept but a material possibility. One can have a body that does not die. This is granted by the Jade Emperor of the heavens to a select few beings, who did something special in their life, thus earning their place amongst the gods.

In the Hindu scriptures, we learn of Vyasa and Markandeya, who are immortal so that they can tell the world stories which contain Vedic wisdom. There is Parashuram, who is immortal so he can observe how violence does not end the problems born of ignorance and ego. There is also Mahabali, who is immortal but allowed to visit his kingdom only once a year to remind all that prosperity, pleasure and power cannot be eternal.

Kripa and Ashwatthama, in the Mahabharata, are immortal so they can remind people of the horrors of war. Vibhishana and Hanuman, in the Ramayana, are immortal to remind people of the story of Ram, the king who never had a happy family life despite being a great king.

Pati-vrata

While male mendicants could outsmart death by being celibate, women acquired similar powers by being faithful to husbands, in Hindu lore. Pati-vrata means one who is faithful to her husband in mind and body. Such a woman is also called Sati. She is the opposite of the sensuous and unchaste apsara, the celestial courtesan. Her chastity made her so powerful that she could defeat death itself.

The earliest such tale linking a wife's chastity to her ability to overpower death comes from the Mahabharata. We learn of a princess called Savitri, who marries a woodcutter called Satyavan. Satyavan is doomed to die a year after his wedding. But when Yama claims the spirit of her husband, Savitri does not let go. She follows him until, impressed by her persistence, Yama offers her a boon, anything but the life of her husband. She then asks that she have children by her dead husband. Yama agrees before he realises the implication, that his boon can only manifest

Devdutt Pattanaik

if the dead husband is given life again. Thus, Yama is tricked into letting Satyavan live.

The story of how Savitri brought her husband back from the land of the dead is narrated by women who want their husbands to live long and healthy lives. They ritually express their desire in an annual Vata-Savitri festival by fasting and tying threads around a banyan tree (akshaya vata), which is assumed to be immortal.

Savitri with Satyavan in the shade of the banyan tree (Vata). The women tie threads around the tree, seeking longevity for their husbands.

The idea of a woman being responsible for the life of her husband became popular in medieval India. This led to the formulation of many observances (vrata) for women, which would ensure that their husbands lived a long and healthy life. For example, in northern India, women observe Karwa Chauth in the autumn season, when they fast all day and look at the moon and their husband's face through a sieve before breaking their fast. In Kerala, women observe Tiruvathira, when they do not eat rice and remember the story of Shilavati, who was so faithful to her husband that she had the power to stop the sun from setting to prevent his death. In Bengal, there are stories of how worshipping the goddess Manasa can help a woman revive her husband after he has been bitten by a venomous snake. In Odisha, women worship Mangala to ensure the safety of their husbands in case of a shipwreck.

In all of these stories, the fidelity of a woman plays a key role in saving her husband from death. We learn of Vrinda, the wife of an Asura called Jalandhara, who is so faithful to her husband that the Devas are unable to defeat him. So, Vishnu takes the form of Jalandhara and visits Vrinda, who serves him as she would serve her husband. Thus she, without knowing it, becomes unfaithful and strips her husband of the protection granted by her chastity, so he can be killed easily. Afterwards, Vrinda curses Vishnu that he will be worshipped as a fossil-stone, the Shaligrama, and herself turns into a tulsi shrub. An apologetic Vishnu declares that henceforth, no worship to him will be complete without the offering of a sprig of tulsi.

Similar stories are to be found in folk versions of the Ramayana.

Ravana's queens desire the virile Hanuman and so are unable to protect Ravana with the power of their chastity. By connecting the wife's fidelity to her husband's mortality, a new reason was found to justify the practice of widow burning. In medieval times, it was declared that a woman who never thought of another man during marriage would never become a widow. So, a widow was essentially one who was not faithful to her husband. And the infidelity need not be physical. Infidelity in thought was bad enough. Renuka had a momentary lapse of self-control and experienced lust for a handsome Gandharva, as a result of which her husband, Rishi Jamadagni, was killed by a king after a dispute.

To prove their fidelity, widows had to burn themselves on their husbands' funeral pyre. If a woman was truly chaste, it was said, she would not feel the heat of the fire or the pain of burning to death. She would travel with her husband to the land of the dead and they would be reborn as a couple for seven generations.

The belief that a woman's fidelity kept her husband alive was clearly a strategy to ensure that women did not seek a relationship outside marriage. In ancient India, merchants travelled from city to city to conduct their trade. In *Suka Saptati*, we hear the story of how, in the absence of one such merchant, his wife wanted to visit her lovers, but was stopped by a wise parrot. If a woman's fidelity kept her husband safe, it also protected her from widowhood, which was seen as the worst fate for a woman in a society that did not permit remarriage.

Ruru, the husband who gave up half his life to resurrect his wife, Pramadvara

Since widowers could remarry, we do not hear Hindu stories of men facing death to save their wives, as in the Greek myth of Orpheus seeking Eurydice. There is one exception, though. The Mahabharata tells the story of a man called Ruru who begs Yama to return his wife, Pramadvara. Yama agrees when Ruru agrees to give his wife half his life.

Ayonija

Those who are born of the womb (yoni) are bound to experience death. The womb is the portal from the land of the dead to the land of the living. But what about those beings who can be born without passing through the womb? These are the ayonija, worshipped as divine, as they are not bound by the rules of death and rebirth. Among them is Sita, who is born of the earth; Draupadi, who is born of fire; Kartikeya, who is born when Shiva's fiery semen is incubated by wind, fire, water, river reeds and stars; and Ganesha, whose body is

Sita, ploughed out of the earth by Janaka. She is ayonija as she did not emerge from a womb

moulded from the dirt of his mother's body and his elephant head is fixed by his father. These are the divine beings who are worshipped in temples.

Vishnu chooses to be a yonija, take birth through the womb and experience birth and death on earth as Ram and Krishna. These are the avatars, the mortal and limited forms of the immortal infinite. Narayana-Vishnu, who lives in Vaikuntha, is always young and immortal, but the Krishna on earth who experiences birth must die, struck by the arrow of a hunter.

Mortality forces us to think about life, about kindness, compassion and dharma. Adharma springs from delusions of immortality, the belief that vast wealth and power will enable us to outsmart death. In the Mahabharata, Yudhishtira, having faced misfortune, and having confronted the truth of the forest, when asked by a yaksha, 'What is the greatest wonder?' replies, 'Each day people die. And the rest live as if they are immortal.' Krishna's death described in the Mahabharata draws attention to this truism.

Swayambhu

God, or Bhagavan, is greater than the Devas and the Asuras. God does not crave immortality or attain immortality. He is Swayambhu, which means self-created. In the Vedas, God is Purusha. In the Brahmanas, he is Prajapati. In the Upanishads, he is Atma. In the Puranas, he is Shiva and Vishnu.

Shiva says he has no ancestors and so does not need children. But Shiva's companions are the preta, who await rebirth. Only with a body can they practise yoga that will help them break the endless cycle of rebirths. So they need the goddess Shakti, embodiment of nature, to provide them with a womb through which they can re-inhabit a body and regain life.

Krishna shot by a hunter. Since he was born of a womb he had to experience death before returning to Vaikuntha.

While the idea of swaymbhu speaks of a god who is never born and never dies, in folk belief all gods die. Only their lifespans are different. Human lifespan is equal to a blink of Indra. Indra's lifespan is equal to Brahma's blink. Brahma's lifespan is equal to Vishnu's blink. Vishnu's lifespan is equal to Shiva's blink. Shiva's lifespan is equal to Devi's blink. No one knows whose blink equals the Devi's lifespan. Infinity is not measurable.

Devdutt Pattanaik

Chapter 10

Facing Death

*In which we learn how death was
embraced, not feared,
in Hindu lore*

Once, there was an Asura called Vritra. To kill him, Indra, king of Devas, needed a weapon made of the hardest material available on earth. These could only be the bones of a hermit, who had no attachment for life. He would give them up voluntarily. A rishi called Dadhichi heard of this and offered his bones. The withdrawal of his senses from the material world had made his bones strong. Withdrawal of life from his body was the next step for him, the ultimate act of detachment. When his spirit had left his body, the gods gathered his bones and fashioned the weapon called Vajra out of it, using which Indra killed Vritra. So, did Dadhichi die by suicide? Can he be called a martyr, one who sacrifices his life for a higher truth? Or did he take samadhi, the yogic practice of voluntarily pushing one's spirit out of one's body?

While hermits encouraged fasting to death as a means of wiping out karmic debt, householders considered the act of suicide wrong as it meant escaping social responsibilities. Yet, we learn of kings, priests, even saints, not to mention widows, who killed themselves voluntarily and earned the respect of their community. This ambiguity is evident in the Upanishads. The Isha Upanishad states, 'Those who take their lives reach after death the sunless regions, covered by impenetrable darkness.' But the Kanthashruti Upanishad allows wise hermits to die voluntarily, by drowning or fire, or by inflicting violence on themselves like heroic beings, or vira. Indian folklore is full of stories of men and women embracing death voluntarily in the form of retirement, renunciation or driven by the belief in death over dishonour.

Retiring from the Household

When the Asuras seek immortality, they are told that this is one boon that cannot be granted. Everyone has to die. So, preparing for death became an important theme in Hindu stories and scriptures. It gave rise to the concept of ashrama-dharma. Life was divided into four parts: in the first part, one prepared for the householder's life; in the second part, one lived the householder's life; in the third part, one withdrew from the householder's life; and in the fourth part, one focused on preparing for death. The first phase was called brahmacharya ashrama, then came grihastha ashrama, vanaprastha ashrama and, finally, sanyasa ashrama.

Vanaprastha ashrama refers to the stage in life when a householder passes on the mantle of family responsibilities to the next generation and proceeds to live in the forest (vana). The forest here is metaphorical. It refers to retirement, an intermediate stage between the life of a householder and a hermit. One gradually gives up dependence and embraces independence. One passes on wealth and power to one's children and knowledge to the grandchildren. This may sound easy in theory but is difficult to practice.

In the Ramayana, we see Dasharatha wanting to give up his throne and retire to the forest so that his son, Ram, can be crowned king. He is thus making way for the next generation. This is dharma. The earth should not be burdened by more than two generations at a time: the growing generation and the grown-up generation. The senior must withdraw and make way for the juniors.

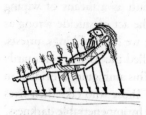

Bhisma was pinned to the ground as he would not let the next generation take decisions

In the Mahabharata, Shantanu does not want to retire. He wants to marry a young woman and restart his life as a householder. His ancestor, Yayati, wants the youth of his children, so that he can keep enjoying life. This is adharma. For

Devdutt Pattanaik

having sacrificed his birthright to please his father, Shantanu's son, Devavrata, renamed Bhishma, was given the gift of choice when it comes to the time of his death. He refused to die until all the problems of his family are resolved. Krishna got him pinned to the ground, immobilised by arrows in the battlefield, so that he could not interfere with the fight of the next generation. Thus, the idea of social death is reinforced. The old must make way for the young. Even Dhritarashtra and Gandhari, parents of the Kauravas, are encouraged by Vidura to give up royal comforts after the death of their children and go to the forest. In the forest, when a fire breaks out and Dhritarashtra wants to run away, Gandhari advises him to sit and accept death.

Renouncing Life

The Dharma-shastra recommends renunciation (sanyasa ashrama) after retirement (vanaprastha ashrama) and the completion of all worldly duties. This is why many people choose to spend their final days in places like Haridwar and Varanasi, on the bank of the river Ganga. They hope to die there and go straight to a higher heaven, bypassing Yama-loka. There are special hostels made in these pilgrim spots for people waiting to die. Similar ideas are found in other pilgrim spots too, like Puri, which is called Swarga-dwar, doorway to paradise.

Some men chose to renounce the world without entering the householder stage. Adi Shankaracharya, who revived interest in Vedanta in the eighth century, was one such man. This practice was encouraged by many monastic orders. Many women chose to be nuns rather than wives.

In the Mahabharata and the Puranas, we find resistance to this idea. Hermits such as Jaratkaru, Kardama and Agastya are tormented by terrifying visions of ancestors hanging upside down from the branch of a tree over a bottomless

Despite current problems (elephant) and future problems (snakes), and the passage of time (white and black rats gnawing at the roots), humans focus on pleasure (honey) rather than escape pit. They are asked to repay debts to ancestors, produce children, before renouncing the world completely. So, Jaratkaru and Kardama take wives and produce children, but walk away from their families soon afterwards. Agastya, however, chooses to embrace the householder's life.

The purpose of renunciation was to withdraw from the quest for wealth, power and pleasure. The point was to reflect on the world, and on life, with the intention of outgrowing all needs and fears. This manifested as indifference to, and detachment from, the world as well as life. It could also involve prayopavesa, or choosing to die by fasting. The hermit was supposed to eat only that which the wind brought him.

The human body was seen as having three layers: the social, the physical and the mental. The social layer comprised wealth, power, estates, titles and relationships. This was given up through the yogic practice of yama and niyama. In yama one focused on withdrawing from others and becoming less dependent, while in niyama one focused on making oneself independent. Yama involved not hurting anyone (ahimsa), not accumulating (aparigraha), not stealing (asteya), not lying (satya), not indulging in sexual activities (brahmacharya) and not judging (daya). Niyama involved being clean (saucha), content (santosh), restrained (tapas), reflective (swadhyay) and having faith (Ishwar-pranidhan). These two practices enabled the householder to become a hermit.

The hermit in a termite hill with creepers around him, indicating total detachment from the external world

The hermit further isolated himself, by training his body to avoid dependence on the external world totally, until the state of isolation (kaivalya) was attained. This was refined in Jain monastic orders giving rise to the practice known as sallekhana or santhara, where monks fasted to death after years of systematic and intense training.

The yogic practice of samadhi enabled the yogi to voluntarily cause his spirit (atma) to leave his body (deha). Such a hermit who seeks independence even from bodily urges does not see anyone or anything. He does not even withdraw from the threat posed by predatory

Devdutt Pattanaik

animals and plants. In art, such a hermit is shown as sitting or standing still, with snakes slithering around his neck, creepers growing on his limbs, covered by a termite hill, or with birds making nests on his head. He is no longer the eater who consumes. He does not fear being eaten, consumed by the world around him. Thus, he abandons all forms of violence, including the violence required to feed and protect himself.

In the Ramayana, after fulfilling his duty, Ram enters the river Sarayu and does not rise again. This act of jala-samadhi was different from suicide. Suicide was seen as violently withdrawing from the world, exhausted by its demands, terrified of the pressures, refusing to fulfil social obligations or face the karmic consequences of past actions. Samadhi was seen as voluntarily getting the spirit to leave the physical body after completing all of one's social duties. Other forms of samadhi included jumping into fire, or simply walking into the forest and giving up food. In the Mahabharata, this is what the Pandavas do when they pass on their kingdom to Parikshit and walk up the mountains in their old age.

About 2,300 years ago, according to folklore, Emperor Chandragupta Maurya lost all interest in the material world during a time of drought. He became a monk and fasted to death. His advisor, Chanakya, hoped to continue his role but Chandragupta's son, Bindusara, did not trust him. Realising that he was no longer valued, and that his social responsibilities were over, Chanakya chose to smoke himself to death by sitting on a pile of burning wood.

Similarly, around 1,300 years ago, Vedanta scholar Kumaril Bhatta decided to withdraw from life by seating himself on a pile of slowly burning wood at the confluence of the Ganga and the Yamuna. Earlier, when his Buddhist teacher had made fun of Vedic rituals, he had decided to jump off a cliff to prove the power of the Vedas. He survived the fall but lost vision in one eye. He realised then that his faith in the Vedas was conditional and faulty, and that he had probably outlived his utility. His ritualistic approach to the Vedas (Mimansa) was inadequate. He had to make way for a new teacher (Adi Shankara) who would bring a better understanding of the Vedas through intuition and intellectual analysis (Vedanta).

Death Before Dishonour

Tamil Sangam literature, which is nearly 2,000 years old, tells us of kings who chose to sit facing north, and fast unto death when defeated in battle or rejected by their people, to uphold their honour in death rather than live on in disgrace. This practice of facing north and dying was called Vatakkiruttal and descriptions of it can be found in many songs in the *Purananuru*. Sometimes, those loyal to the king would join them. For instance, after the death of King Vel Pari in battle, his poet-friend Kapilar gave up his life in this manner.

In another account, King Kopperuncholan's sons fight him for the throne, and even raise an army against him. As the king prepares for battle, his advisors ask him if it is worth going to war. 'If you lose, they will rejoice in your defeat. If you win, who will you leave your kingdom to? You will have no heirs.' The king then decides to face north and fast unto death. He invites his favourite poets to die with him. 'Fetch the poet who lives in the south. I cannot die without him. He who stayed away from me in fortune will surely join me in misfortune.' Some of the

Heroic beheading of the self

poets arrive too late. 'The world praised you when you gave them shade. But you could not complete your reign. You are reduced to a small space, an undecaying stone. The other stones here will give me space. I come to them with an old love, the one that holds me to them as life to a body.' There were other poets who were heartbroken that they had not been invited. 'On the river-island, in spotted shade, you sit, and your body shrivels. Are you angry with me, warrior, that you ask others to join you here? Not me.'

The idea of death before dishonour is a common theme in warrior communities. The more violent stories are those from medieval Rajput communities, which inform us about the practice of Jauhar, or women burning themselves to death to avoid capture by enemies. These women were worshipped as goddesses. There are also stories of men who killed themselves before the image of a god, when defeat seemed inevitable. Anything was preferable to life in disgrace.

In one legend linked with the king of Ranthambore, a Rajput king called Hammir gives shelter to a soldier who has incurred the wrath of a Delhi Sultan. This angers the Delhi Sultan, who attacks the king's fort with a massive army. Even after many wars, and losing many soldiers, when defeat appears inevitable, the king refuses to break his promise to the soldier and chooses to die instead. The royal women are told to immolate themselves. His minister then sacrifices nine elephants to Shiva-Bhairava to remind all of how the sacrifice of Hammir must be seen as Ravana sacrificing his ten heads to Shiva. Thus, his honourable death was transformed into an act of devotion.

Death as Devotion

Stone sculptures found in Telangana, Andhra Pradesh, Karnataka and Tamil Nadu, from the Chola to the Vijayanagar period (from the fifth to the fifteenth century), show images of young men who offered their own head or cut open their guts to expose the entrails, as an act of courage and devotion in honour of a king or a god. This brought them immortality and eternal fame. The families of these men were given land in their memory, prompting many such sacrifices. And while kings gave land to the men who gave up their bodies to display loyalty, the gods gave them access to secret knowledge.

The legendary king Vikramaditya cut off his head and offered it to the goddess Kali, to earn her love and blessings. She was so pleased that she resurrected him and revealed to him the Tantric secrets of life, death and longevity. He understood that he could double the duration of his rule if he spent half his life as a householder and half as a hermit. So Vikramaditya shared his kingdom with his brother, Bhartrihari, who also did the same. While one brother lived as a hermit, the other was householder-king. By alternating their rule, the two brothers governed their kingdom for a very long time. This longevity was also linked to celibacy. As hermits, they stayed away from sensual

A devotee offering his head to the Goddess

pleasures. As householder-kings, they enjoyed sensual pleasures. As hermits, they gathered power. As householders, they expended power. This knowledge came to Vikramaditya through self-sacrifice.

While there are hero-stones that commemorate warriors who have laid down their lives to protect people, land or cattle, there are also memorials to heroes who offered their head, perhaps symbolically, to a god or a king, to express loyalty and devotion, or to receive honour and fame. The tenth-century Tamil ballad *Kalingattuparani* states, 'Like the roaring sound of ocean waves, the shouts of heroes offering their heads in return for the bestowal of boons were echoing all over the area.'

In Tamil Nadu's Terukuttu performances of the Mahabharata, Aravan, Arjuna's son by Ulupi, is asked to offer himself as a human sacrifice to the goddess Kali to ensure victory for his father. He does this, but only after he is given a wife. For he wishes to experience conjugal pleasure at least once before he dies. He also wants someone to truly mourn him when he is gone. Since no woman wants to marry a man doomed to die at sunrise, Krishna turns into the damsel Mohini and marries him. They spend the night as husband and wife, and in the morning, she mourns his sacrifice as his widow.

Atop many Hindu temples one sees the image of a severed head. Similar images are found on arches placed behind images of deities. This head is called kirti-mukha, the head of glory. Kirti-mukha was a Shiva-gana, or follower of Shiva, who was very hungry but refused to eat others and so decided to eat his own body. To live, he chose to consume himself rather than consume others. His offering of oneself to oneself was the ultimate act of devotion. His head atop temples and arches, often with tongue sticking out and baring fangs, is to remind all devotees that as long as they consume others, their devotion is an act of self-delusion.

Chapter 11

Ending Death

*In which we learn how Hindus
imagined liberation from
the wheel of rebirths*

Parikshit was bitten by a snake and was doomed to die in a week's time. He wondered what was the point of a life cut so prematurely. Shuka-muni, the parrot-headed son of Vyasa, came to the dying king and told him the story of Krishna, who was God-on-earth. Krishna also had to die, accidentally shot by the poison-tipped arrow of a hunter. Before dying, he had given the wisdom of life and death to Uddhava, his old friend. He spoke of two possibilities after death: rebirth or liberation from rebirths. The idea of eternal afterlife based on God's judgment is alien to Hindu thought.

Moksha, or liberation from rebirths, involves oblivion (nirvana) of the self in Buddhism, and isolation (kaivalya) of the self in Jainism; in Hinduism it involves union (yoga) of the self with God or the cosmic spirit. In Vedanta, the cosmic spirit is referred to as the impersonal 'Param-atma', 'Brahman' or 'Purusha'. With the rise of theism, words like Bhagavan and Ishwar began to be used instead, to make the cosmic spirit appear more sentient, sensitive and compassionate.

Entrapment in the cycle of samsara by Kaal-Bhairava, the fearsome lord of time. The noose binds us. The elephant-goad (ankush) is meant to pull and prod us. The flames indicate hunger that consumes us.

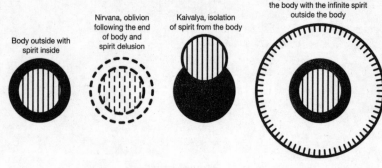

Liberation in karmic traditions

In bhakti literature, the cosmic spirit is embodied as Shiva, Vishnu or the Goddess. So, liberation is visualised as reaching the abode of Shiva, Vishnu or the Goddess, and staying there permanently. The Garuda Purana focuses on devotion to Vishnu, but also refers to ideas from the Upanishads and the Dharma-shastra that predate theism. Union with the divine, in the Hindu scheme of things, is achieved in three ways:

1. Gyan-marga: the intellectual path of the hermit

2. Karma-marga: the practical path of the householder

3. Bhakti-marga: the emotional path of the devotee

The Hermit's Knowing

In the Gita, which is a dialogue in the epic Mahabharata, Krishna speaks of the atma which never dies. In Vedanta literature, atma is described as a being without form (nirakar), shape (nirupa), qualities (nirguna) or divisions (akhand), unbound by time (akaal), eternal (nitya) and tranquil (sadananda), and a witness to life (sakshi). When Krishna reveals his cosmic form, with infinite heads and infinite limbs, that consumes and generates infinite worlds, one sees that there are no boundaries, divisions or hierarchies. He shows us how the limitless Narayana is no different from the limited Krishna. He knows this, but Arjuna has forgotten. Krishna tells Arjuna that his insecurities and doubts stem from this forgetfulness. And the forgetfulness stems from attachment. He needs to break the vicious cycle of forgetfulness and attachment.

We feel we are alone in the world. We need nourishment (anna) and security (abhaya). We crave pleasure (sukkha) and shun pain (dukkha). We get angry and frustrated when we do not get what we seek, jealous when others have what we want. We fight to get what we want and cling to what we gather. Ignorance entraps us further in the wheel of rebirths. It keeps making us crave for things, regret failure and fear loss. The wise neither yearn nor regret. Neither do they fear. They enjoy life and accept death without clinging to anything or anyone.

Most of us spend our lives accumulating wealth, property, power, estates, titles, relationships, even knowledge. This creates a new body—a cultural body—around our natural body, made of all that we possess. We do not like to share this cultural body. Before we die, we ensure that all that we possess goes to those we consider as ours. And when we die, our ghost leaves our body. But this ghost is not free. It is trapped by debts; it has to repay and reclaim. For it has spent its lifetime consuming and clinging. These debts are the karmic burden that eclipses the jiva-atma, like covering a crystal with dust and dirt. These debts drown us in ignorance. They turn the jiva-atma into preta.

The wise know that ignorance as well as wisdom are embodied in the flesh. Our flesh can take many forms: that of trees, animals, birds and fishes. Our flesh obscures our access to wisdom, like the eclipse blocks the sun.

In ignorance, we keep discarding old bodies and gaining new bodies, again and again and again. After eighty-four hundred thousand (84,00,000) births, we obtain the human flesh which has the wherewithal to discover that embodied wisdom. Unfortunately, it is distracted by craving, like a fish distracted by the meat on the sharp end of a fisherman's hook.

The human body is a special gift. It contains everything that can help us break free from the wheel of rebirths. We must nourish it and protect it from disease. We cannot stop it from ageing, and it will experience accidents

Krishna's cosmic form containing the killer and the killed

and ailments from time to time. But as long as we are healthy, we must seek the wisdom embodied within it diligently and before it is too late. Do not wait till old age and the moments before death to think about wisdom, like that man who digs a well, looking for water, when his house is burning.

No one knows when they will die. Yet, enchanted by joys and trapped in miseries, they rarely think about wisdom. The wealthy, the healthy, the fortunate forget how quickly things can turn bad. The poor, the unfortunate, the diseased yearn for good times and contemplate no further. Drunk on the delusions of joy and sorrow, no one thinks about the hereafter. A life spanning one hundred years is hardly enough time. Half of it is lost sleeping. Half of our waking hours are overtaken by stress, ailments and conflicts, and the rest in anxieties and ambitions. Life is like sea foam. Fragile. Momentary. But no one thinks about imminent death. With time, even Mount Meru withers away, the unbaked pot dissolves in water.

Death claims family and friends and, continuously, relentlessly, it gnaws at the living, yet we are busy with our tasks, fighting for things, clinging to things, mourning the loss of things. We have been enchanted by the magic of thirst, hunger, sensory delights, emotional yearnings, attractions and revulsions. The world is forever changing, it is the root of all sorrow, yet we do not pause to reflect upon it. A man in jail is eventually released, but not a man entrapped by social relationships. All creatures crave food, sex, comfort, power and sleep. But if that is all man craves, then how is he different from bird, beast or tree? What differentiates humans is knowledge about death and freedom, embedded within and awaiting discovery. Foolish is the man who is driven by the call of nature every morning, by hunger and thirst every day, by pleasure and sleep every night. The wise cultivate detachment. To cultivate detachment, one needs to surround oneself with people who are refined, those whose eyes can separate milk from water, like the mythical goose.

As per folklore, to escape imminent defeat in Kurukshetra, Duryodhan floated across a river of blood, oblivious to the fact that he was clinging to the corpse of his own son. Such is human attachment to mortal life.

Devdutt Pattanaik

We should be asking ourselves why we use words like 'mine' and 'not mine' in our daily lives. Where does this division come from? The 'mine' binds us, the 'not mine' liberates us. The more we pursue 'mine', the more we fetter ourselves, fill ourselves with anxiety and entrap ourselves with fleeting sensory experiences. From this idea of 'mine' comes restlessness, pride, contempt, rage, jealousy, hatred. Those who let go are able to calm down, see the truth and are able to understand death, as well as life, with grace and dignity. For nothing belongs to anyone. All that is grabbed will be left behind. All that is remembered will be forgotten.

In gyan-marga, one appreciates the pull of the sense-horses and the mind-chariot, and recognises the self within that gives value to all the things it consumes while creating boundaries and hierarchies, as well as concepts such as mine and not mine, which, in turn, result in attachment, revulsion and fear of death. This is what stops us from being generous with words, with actions, with wealth, which makes us cling to things and to thoughts, even to breath. But those who taste the spiritual nectar are no longer interested in material feasts. They stop craving and regretting, envying and denying. They share everything freely. They let go of everything effortlessly.

When one breaks free from attachment, judgement, liking and disliking, loving and hating, when one is truly generous, materially and emotionally, one can sit anywhere and be liberated enough to welcome death without fear. There is no yearning for paradise or fear of hell, no aspiration or terror, just peace. This is moksha, according to the Garuda Purana.

The Householder's Doing

In the Garuda Purana, Vishnu tells Garuda that those who wish to end repeated births and repeated deaths need to find the truly refined, the authentic. Avoid the imposter who performs rituals, who does not see the big picture. Avoid those who are obsessed with ceremonies but do not appreciate the meaning, who fast and torture the body but fail to refine the mind. Avoid those who wear animal skin, mat their hair, smear their body with ash and mouth Vedic axioms while enjoying the temporary pleasures of the material world, competing with other ascetics for fame and glory. Donkeys walk around naked, but that does not make them wise; walking naked does not make you wise. Dogs roll on ash, but that does not make them wise; smearing your body with ash does not make you wise. Deer eat grass, but that does not make them wise; eating grass does not make you wise. Fish live in the Ganga, but that does not make them wise; merely living next to the Ganga does not make you wise. Rituals and practices are not ends in themselves. They simply increase the probability of insight into wisdom.

Simply memorising the Vedas, studying the Shastras, chanting hymns and sacred texts does not make anyone wise. Knowledge is not enough. Observe those who are learned in poetry, or the best of grammarians and logicians, and notice the anxiety that consumes them. They are not wise. Those who argue viciously over the truth do not know the truth, just as a spoon carrying honey does not know what sweetness is. Memorisation does not grant you wisdom, just as talking about lamps does not take away the darkness. Knowledge is infinite and it will take infinite lifetimes to gather all knowledge. But insight comes in a flash, a moment, if one is keen. And once that insight is obtained, there is no need for scriptures or rituals or performance. They are like stalks of grass after the grain has been threshed.

Wisdom is the realisation that you are not alone in the world. The world is neither the prey that you crave nor the predator that you fear. You too are prey for someone else, and also a predator. The jiva-atma (self) thus empathises with the para-atma (the other), recognises how the other thinks and feels in hunger, fear and ignorance. Everything that lives in this world is both eater and eaten. Trees, plants, animals, humans, even gods and demons, sages and sorcerers, ghosts and ancestors. Alone, they feel like victims, fear villains and seek heroes. But when they realise that they are not alone, that there is no separation between self and other, that everyone is part of an ecosystem, the story changes. Instead of eating and being eaten, they strive to feed and be fed.

The wedding rite of passage (vivaha samskara) to enable the return of the previous generation as the next generation

Eaters and eaten establish samsara, which is nature. Culture is about the feeders and the fed, and this is established through samskara, or rites of passage. The sound 'ka' distinguishes samsara (nature) from samskara (cultural activities). In Hindu funeral rituals, the mashed rice balls for the dead are offered to crows to eat. Why crows? Many explanations are offered. One states that crows make the sound 'ka', which in Sanskrit is the sound of interrogation. For example, in Hindi, 'ka' gives rise to words for what (kya), when (kab), where (kahan), how (kaise) and why (kyon). An examined life is an indicator of how cultured we are.

All organisms act to survive. But humans know that they live in an ecosystem of debt. Repayment of what we owe others liberates us. In samskara, you focus on the hunger and fear of others.

- You produce children to help ancestors. This begins with garbha-dana samskara for conception and ends with nama-karana samskara for naming the child.

- You feed children until they can feed themselves. This is marked by anna-prasanna samskara when you feed the child, the chuda-karma samskara when you cut their hair and the karna-bheda samskara when you pierce their ears, and thus transform them from beasts to humans.

- You ensure that your children, like you, do their duty (sva-dharma) based on their lineage (varna-dharma) and stage of life (ashrama-dharma), adequately modified in calamitous times (apad-dharma).

- You teach your children that they, like you, exist for the generation as providers of knowledge (brahmana), security (kshatriya), goods (vaishya) and services (shudra). You teach them the value of exchange (yagna) and generosity (daan).

- You educate children to prepare them for the world. This is brahmacharya ashrama, which begins with vidya-arambha samskara and continues with the upanayana samskara, when the child is ready to appreciate how he is part of a co-dependent ecosystem of family, friends, strangers, culture, nature, ghosts and ancestors.

- You get children married to help them repay their debts to ancestors, to family, culture and nature. This is grihastha-ashrama, which begins with vivaha samskara.

- You withdraw from the world when your children are ready. This is vanaprastha ashrama.

- You withdraw from life when you are ready. This is sanyasa ashrama.

- When you die, you hope your family will perform the antyeshti and the shradh, to help your ghost make its journey to Pitr-loka.

By engaging with the other (para-atma), you realise the infinite (param-atma). And by realising the infinite, you realise the delusion (maya) of boundaries, divisions and hierarchies. You do not see the other merely as opportunity or threat, to be consumed or feared. You realise that ultimately you are just like everything and everyone else—food.

The Devotee's Feeling

As Vedic Hinduism transformed into Puranic Hinduism from 1000 BCE to 500 CE, concepts such as nirguna-brahman (divine without form), the saguna-brahman (divine with form) and avatar (divine on earth) emerged. The abstract was thus made concrete. The limitless was made limited. The mysterious divine became accessible. The accessible divine took the form of icons that were enshrined in temples. These were approached as a man approaches a leader or teacher or master. This submission to authority was popular with kings and encouraged by them and became widespread with the rise of states.

In Hindu temples, gods were increasingly shown engaged with the material world and solving material problems: there was Shiva, who married Shakti and descended from Kailasa to serve as sheriff (kotwal) of Kashi; there was the four-armed Vishnu, who became the two-armed Ram and Krishna of Ayodhya and Mathura who had to contend with tyrants like Ravana and Jarasandha; and there was Durga, the daughter of Brahma, the sister of Vishnu and the wife of Shiva, who fought enemies in battle and fed the hungry at home.

Shiva rescuing Markandeya from Yama

The Puranas spoke of eternal heavens such as Kailasa, the abode of Shiva, and Vaikuntha, the abode of Vishnu. Looking at God's image (darshan), hearing their stories (sravana), thinking about them (smarana) and adoring them through ritual (puja-archana-upasana) was enough to break the cycle of rebirths.

In bhakti literature, the dead do not have to suffer the horrors of Yama-loka or the bleakness of Pitr-loka. If they worship Shiva, they will land up in Kailasa, where there is no hunger. If they worship Vishnu, they will reach Vaikuntha, on the ocean of milk. If they worship Krishna, they will end up in Go-loka, where Krishna plays his flute eternally under the wish-fulfilling tree, surrounded by wish-fulfilling cows. This is the bhakti-marga, or path of devotion.

Devotees of Shiva told stories of how Markandeya was saved from Yama's noose by Shiva himself when he clung to the Shiva-linga like a baby monkey clinging to his mother for safety. They spoke of how a thief landed up in Kailasa because, while escaping from some guards, he climbed a bilva tree and accidentally caused the leaves, much loved by Shiva, to fall on a Shiva-linga.

Devotees of Vishnu told stories of how Ajamila, the gambler and scoundrel, was saved from Yama's messengers by Vishnu's messengers because he called out his son's name before dying. This name, Narayana, happened to be Vishnu's too. Ajamila is often compared to a lost irresponsible kitten carefully taken to safety by the mother cat. Vishnu devotees also narrated the story of how Vishnu answered the prayers of his devotee, the elephant-king Gajendra, and rescued him from the jaws of a crocodile in a lotus pond, a metaphor for how prayer liberates us from the sensory trap of materialism.

Vishnu-duta rescuing Ajamila from Yama-duta

In many parts of India, devotees preferred the divine embodied in a human form rather than in images and icons. For them, a charismatic guru became the master, a medium for God. Unlike the gurus of Vedic times, who were simply teachers and instructors, a new type of guru became prominent in India after the tenth century. These gurus were seen as embodiments of the divine, fountainheads of energy, to be adored and worshipped. The idea of submission to a doctrine was perhaps influenced by the rising popularity of the concept of Almighty, all-merciful God and God's messenger that was reaching India through Christian and Muslim traders, warlords and missionaries. Today, devotees sing chants that place a guru above teachers, above gods, above parents. Devotees give their wealth to the guru, outsource all decisions to the guru, surrender totally to the whims of the guru. This feels like liberation.

Devdutt Pattanaik

Conclusion

*In which we learn why the
Hindu world view does not have the
concept of Judgement Day*

When people die, most people around the world say RIP, which is short for Rest in Peace. This is based on the belief that death is a destination, the end, no moving forward or going back. Lately, many Hindus on social media have given this a Sanskrit spin, saying 'Om Shanti', which is an invocation to peace. This takes away the restlessness and dynamism of the Hindu belief in the afterlife, which is based on the movement of the disembodied ghost from the land of the living to the land of the dead, and its return at the time of rebirth. By feeding the dead, we help the ghost travel in peace, and remind ourselves of hunger, that primal force that drives us to live each day. Travel in Peace, or TIP, would be a more appropriate Hindu acronym.

The resting in RIP occurs in purgatory, the time between the end of an individual's life and the end of the world itself, after which all souls will be judged simultaneously by God. This grand climax is a part of the Christian and Islamic eschatology, that is, myths related to the end. Here the belief is that we live only one life. So, we are expected to live as per God's laws, as revealed by God's messengers or prophets. After death, we wait until Judgement Day ('Qayamat' in Persian) when God decides our fate based on our conduct. The wait is long for the wicked and short for the good. Those who have lived in law and love (halal) will go to Heaven (Jannat); the rest, who disregarded law and love (haram), will be cast into Hell (Jahannum). Those who repent may be shown mercy.

Hindu mythology is very different. There is no waiting in purgatory. There is no Judgement Day. Life, death and rebirth is governed by hunger (kama) and its consequences (karma). Hunger makes us eat. Karma ensures that the eater gets eaten. Humans seek to escape the fate of being eaten by feeding others and earning merit. Those who have not fed others when alive suffer and starve in Naraka after death. Those who have fed others when alive go to Swarga and are fed by the gods. Those who are free of debt and immersed in the divine rise to a higher heaven beyond the wheel of rebirths.

The difference in how Hindus look at death impacts how Hindus look at life:

- Evil, or absence of the divine, is a word that cannot be translated into any Indian language. The closest we get is wicked or evil. There is no concept of the Devil, or demon. The Asuras and Rakshasas are sons of Brahma, just like the Devas. They may be insecure and nasty, but no one is evil. Everyone is part of God, whose inclusive cosmic form is shown to Arjuna in the Bhagavad Gita.

- Sin, or the breaking of God's law, is often translated as paap in Indian languages. But the concept of punya, or positive karma, does not have an equivalent in English or Arabic. Either you follow the rules (halal) or you do not (haram). The approach is binary. The Hindu approach is a number line. The more paap you do, the more negatives you accumulate. The more punya you do, the more positives you accumulate. The number zero is the point that grants liberation from possibilities of rebirth, from all possible heavens and hells.

- The Hindu idea of rebirth implies that no one is born with a clean slate. At birth we carry the burden of past lives, and in death we carry forward the burdens of the current life. This explains inequality and diversity in the world. We cannot simply blame the rich and the powerful; we have to take responsibility too. Generosity is not the burden only of the rich. That we have a human birth makes us elite and privileged, with the wherewithal to discover the divine.

Devdutt Pattanaik

- When you live once, the value of your life is the sum total of achievements as the denominator of your life is one. But when you live infinite lives, the denominator of your life is infinity and so the value of your life, no matter what you do, is zero.

The Middle East, which includes Arabia, Persia, Mesopotamia and Egypt, is the region that gave rise to the one-life mythology that went on to influence Judaism, Christianity and Islam. The Indian subcontinent is where the idea of rebirth emerged, as a part of Jainism, Buddhism and Hinduism. India and the Middle East have had trading relations since Harappan times. Both were aware of the concept of debt. Middle Eastern stories spoke of debts accumulated in a single life; this gave rise to the idea of sin. Indian myths spoke of debts accumulated in multiple lives; this gave rise to the idea of karma. Different stories of death shaped understandings of kindness and compassion, fairness and justice in different cultures. Why did humans create these stories?

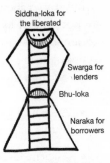

Siddha-loka for the liberated

Swarga for lenders

Bhu-loka

Naraka for borrowers

Jain understanding of the cosmos

Nature does not expect any animal or tree to be kind or compassionate, fair or just. Humans may attribute these qualities to nature through fables, but nature appears indifferent, ruthless, with no favourites. Balance in nature happens on a wider scale, at a species level, not at an individual level. Nature is full of predators and prey, not villains or victims. Everything in nature has an expiry date. But humans have imagination—and that creates ideas about the future, about never dying, about endlessly returning. This imagination propels us towards culture, where we generate food for ourselves, and towards civilisation where we exchange food with others. With production and exchange come the concepts of fairness and justice. Am I being treated the same as others? Am I getting what is due?

The need to be treated fairly and justly is a cultural need, which is expressed and enforced through myths. For example, eagles eating serpents is no crime in nature, but in culture, we want to see one as the victim and the other as villain. So, in the story of Garuda, the Nagas are called tricksters and enslavers of birds, transforming Garuda's need to eat them into an act of justice. When humans kill humans, we need a justification to differentiate ourselves from beasts. We need to clarify that those who kill are heroes and those who are killed are villains, savages and monsters, threats to culture, civilisation, order or progress.

But stories about death need to be supernatural, and have forces that are not limited by death. That is why humans have always composed stories about stern judges and strict accountants, as well as wise and compassionate gods in the afterlife, who are themselves not subject to death. We find these in all cultures.

- Ancient Egyptians spoke of hearts being weighed against the feather of justice by the dog-headed Anubis.

- Ancient Greeks spoke of meaningless repetitive punishments in Tartarus for those who angered the gods.

- Vikings spoke of those who died bravely in battle and were taken to the Halls of Valhalla, by Valkyries, to dine with and fight beside the gods.

- Zoroastrians spoke of a bridge across the fires of hell that becomes narrower for the wicked and wider for the good.

- Jewish, Christian and Islamic lore spoke of the almighty, merciful God as the ultimate judge.

- Hindus spoke of tortures in Naraka that await those who follow adharma, the joys of Swarga for those who follow dharma and a higher heaven for those who follow the path of yoga, when given a second chance of life through rebirth.

Many argue that all these fictions are designed to exploit, that Egyptian pyramids and Mesopotamian tombs enabled the powerful to enslave the peasants, that Hindu funeral rites were designed to benefit Brahmin communities while stripping the Chandala of dignity, that Judgement Day was simply meant to legitimise warfare, enforce standardisation and wipe out creativity. They believe progress demands a rejection of all stories and the creation of impersonal institutions that enable a rational redistribution of material wealth and power.

Unfortunately, such a world exists only in the imagination: a world

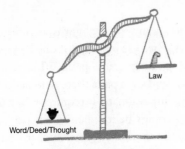

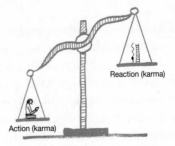

The Egyptian balance is based on the standard universal scale: heart weighed against the feather of justice (standard measurement)

Yama's balance (dharma-kanta) is based on the relative proportion scale: the fate (karma) that you receive is equal to the action (karma) that you gave

where humans are so rational that they are kind and generous of their own volition. Modern 'rational' myths of revolution and nation-state offer the delusion of a happily ever after, sometime in the future, provided everyone is in agreement. So, the present is spent arguing, debating and fighting. Rabid rationalists are now realising how excessive cynicism and the rejection of myths only lead to anarchy. Hegemony, or the use of stories to gain compliance through belief rather than violence, is a necessary tool of culture and civilisation.

An objective scientific study of the vast expanse of the cosmos leaves us feeling stripped of value. We realise we do not matter in the grand scheme of things. Nature does not treat humans any different from a plant or an animal simply because we designed a radical technology or amassed vast amounts of wealth or enslaved entire continents. The most talented and desirable person in the world is no different from a shrub in the forest that is infested with termites. Everyone has an expiry date. No one notices their disappearance. But such a perspective is not good for one's mental health. It leads to depression or, even worse, sociopathy!

The subjective self yearns for value, meaning and purpose. Self-help gurus encourage the elite to leave behind a legacy. This feels ridiculous when we realise that, as a species, humans have existed for over 3,00,000 years. We began farming only 10,000 years ago, and no one remembers the first farmer. No one remembers the tree that bore the sweet mango we ate earlier in the day. We do not even remember what we ate for our last meal, let alone the person who cooked it. But the horror of being forgotten terrifies us. We want to stop thinking, immerse ourselves in tasks. Or we surrender to religious books and spiritual gurus who think for us, tell us what to do, and grant us peace in exchange for obedience.

Meaning gives us pleasure. Meaninglessness causes pain. While there is a natural motivation to seek pleasure and shun pain, there is no natural motivation to be just, fair, caring or compassionate. It requires effort to empathise with others, value other people's beliefs, behaviour, person and property. Myths about death and the afterlife do precisely that. They are shortcuts: simple cultural tools to nudge humans towards empathy, make them care for others through an unconscious reflex rather than a thought-through and rational response.

Humans need stories to cope with life. We need to accept this. We also need to accept that different cultures have different stories. Conflict takes place when one story is privileged over others, when RIP is assumed to be more real than TIP. No scientist, no mystic, no philosopher knows what really happens after we die. But to live enthusiastically, we need a story about death. And to be at peace, we must accept that others may not agree with our story because they have a story of their own.

Devdutt Pattanaik

Glossary

Abhaya	Security, no fear
Abhyudaya-shradh	Feeding the ancestors at a family celebration, such as marriage
Aghori	Occult sorcerers who wander in burial, cremation and charnel grounds.
Aham	Ego; a sense of self at the cost of others
Ahimsa	Non-violence
Akaal	Beyond time
Akhand	Without divisions
Akshaya-patra	Cornucopia
Akshya	Non-decaying
Amangala	Inauspicious, bringing bad luck
Amrita	Nectar of immortality
Amrita-manthan	Churning of the nectar of immortality from the ocean of milk
Antim kriya/sanskar	Last rites
Antyeshti	Funeral rites
Anustarani	Animal slaughtered and its parts spread over the deceased at the time of the funeral in Vedic times
Apad-dharma	Choices in dire situations
Aparigraha	Not accumulating stuff
Apsara	Dancer in paradise, nymph, damsel
Arhat	A hermit-teacher
Ashrama-dharma	Functioning as per stage in life
Asteya	Not stealing
Asthi-visarjan	Immersing bones and ash in river, pond or sea
Asu	Early Vedic term for life force

Ativahika	Temporary subtle body that the preta gets when it leaves the body
Atma	The supreme divine in the Upanishads
Avahan	Invitation
Ayonija	Not born of the womb
Azrael	Angel of death in Islamic mythology
Besnu	Memorial to the dead, a term used in Gujarat
Bhairava	Fierce form of Shiva who wanders amongst funeral pyres
Bhuta	A trapped ghost, unable to travel to the land of dead
Bhuta-daivam	Spirit of the ancestor worshipped as a deity in South Karnataka
Bhuta-kolam	Folk ritual theatre for invoking the spirit-ancestor-gods
Bhuta-pati	Lord of ghosts, a title for Shiva
Brahma-rakshasa	Trapped ghost of a corrupt Brahmin
Brahmacharya ashrama	Stage of a student
Brahman	Vedic term for the power of language, divine spirit, animating force of cosmos
Buddha-loka	The realm of the Buddha in Buddhist mythology
Buddhi	Intelligence, seat of decisions
Chakras	Nodes of the body controlling physiology
Chamunda	The goddess of crematoriums who rides ghosts and eats decaying flesh
Chandalas	Caretakers of the funeral pyre, remover of corpses
Chautha	Memorial to the dead, term used in North India
Chhatri	Pavilion raised over royal Rajput cremation site
Chinta-mani	Wish-fulfilling jewel
Chitta	Heart, the seat of emotions
Chuda-karma samskara	Rite of passage to cut the hair of a newborn for the first time
Dakini	Occult priestess, goddess, expert
Daya	Compassion
Deha	Flesh
Dehi	Resident of flesh, that is, atma
Dhatu	Tissue, mineral, metal
Dukkha	Pain

Devdutt Pattanaik

Ekodishta-shradh	A funeral ritual devoted to a single person, the recently deceased, as opposed to all ancestors
Gandharva	Musicians of paradise
Ganika	Courtesan
Garbha-dana samskara	Rite of passage to mark sexual intercourse aimed at conception
Grihastha ashrama	Stage of householder
Gyan-indriya	Organs that sense (eye, ear, nose, skin, tongue)
Halahala	Poison churned out of the ocean of milk along with the nectar of immortality
Ida	The lunar channel that cools the body
Ishwar-pranidhan	Faith in divine
Jatana deha	Temporary body of the preta
Jiva	Organism
Jivaputrik	The performer of the shradh ritual whose father is alive
jivo jivatsya jivanam	Vedic phrase meaning 'life feeds on life'
Kailasa	Abode of Shiva where no one is hungry
Kaivalya	Jain term for liberation when spirit isolates itself from all things material
Kala	Time
Kalpa	Lifespan of the world, between two floods of doom
Kalpa-taru/Kalpa-vriksha	A wish-fulfilling tree found in paradise
Kama	Desire
Kama-dhenu	Wish-fulfilling cow
Kama-shastra	Erotic manual
Kapalika	Fierce form of Shiva who carries the severed head of Brahma
Karma-indriya	Organs that act (face, head, feet, genitals, anus)
Karna-bheda samskara	Rite of passage to pierce the ear of a newborn for the first time
Karta	Performer of the shradh ritual
Kashi	Holy city, famous for its cremation ground, where the river Ganga turns north for some distance
Kinnara	Singers of paradise; half-bird
Kirti-mukha	Face of glory placed atop temple gates and towers
Koshas	Layers of the body
Kshaya	Decay

Mahatmya	A great chronicle related to a deity or a pilgrim spot
Mana	Mind, seat of thoughts
Mangala	Auspicious, bringing good luck
Matha	Hindu monastic order
Mazaar	Islamic funeral mound raised over the burial spot of a holy man (pir)
Moha	Attachment
Moksha	Liberation from physical needs and the wheel of rebirths
Mukha-agni	Lighting the funeral pyre
Mukti	Freedom from social responsibilities
Mukti-dham	Colloquial phrase for cremation ground
Nadi	Nerves, channels of the body
Nama-karana samskara	Rite of passage to name the newborn
Nandan-kanan	Garden of delights located in paradise
Nandimukha-pitr	Ancestors who are considered auspicious
Naraka	Hell, full of torments
Narayana-bali	Special feeding of the dead, who are ignored, forgotten or unhappy
Nirakar	Without shape
Nirguna	Formless, attribute-less
Nirupa	Without form
Nirvana	Buddhist term for liberation when there is no dependence on the delusion of permanence
Nitya	Eternal
Nityasumangali	Courtesan who has many husbands and so is never a widow
Niyoga	Letting the wife go to another man to bear a child as the husband can't make her pregnant
Pallippadai	Temple built over royal burial or cremation site
Parakaya pravesh	Occult practice of leaving one's body and entering and animating the dead body of another
Parvana-shradh	Standard public ritual of feeding the dead during festivals
Patala	Nether regions below the ground
Pati-vrata	Faithful to husband

Pinda	Ball of mashed rice and sesame that represents the body of, and food for, ancestors
Pinda-daan	Offering of food to ancestors
Pingala	The solar channel that warms the body
Pir	Holy man in Islam
Pishacha	Old ignored ghost that torments the recently dead
Pitr	Ancestors
Pitr-paksha	Fortnight of ancestors
Pitra-hrinn	Debt to ancestors repaid by producing children
Prajapati	The supreme divine in Vedic ritual manuals known as Brahmana
Pralaya	Flood that marks the end of the world before its rebirth
Preta	Ghost; spirit after it leaves the dead body
Preta-shila	A stone in the crematorium where the ghost of the recently deceased awaits
Punar-janma	Rebirth in the cycle of life
Punar-mrityu	Re-death in the cycle of life
Purusha	The supreme divine in the Rig Veda
Qayamat	Judgement Day in Islamic mythology
Rasayana	Alchemy
Sadananda	Always tranquil
Sadhava	Married woman whose husband is alive
Saguna	Embodied, full of attributes
Sakshi	Witness
Sallekhana	Withdrawal from life, hence food, and fasting to death as part of Jain monastic practice
Samadhi	A mound marking the site where a saint chose death or contains relics of the saint
Samashan-bhoomi	Cremation ground
Samsara	The endless cycle of birth and death in the material world
Samskara	The cultured life based on rites of passage
Santhara	Withdrawal from life and food; fasting to death as part of Jain monastic practice
Santosh	Contentment
Sanyasa ashrama	Stage of renunciation as one prepares for death
Sapinda-karana	Ritual of merging the ghost into the first-generation ancestor

Sarva-pitr	The collective of ancestors
Sati maharani	Widow who burns herself on the funeral pyre of her dead warrior husband and attains the status of goddess
Saucha	Cleanliness, hygiene, both physical and mental
Shaman	A member of a tribe who communicates with spirits of the dead
Sharira	Body
Shava sadhana	Ritual involving dead bodies to obtain occult power
Shradh	Post-funeral rituals
Shradh-bhog	Post-funeral feats
Shunya	Nothingness, zero, a Buddhist concept
Siddha-loka	The realm of the Tirthankara in Jain mythology
Smara	Memory
Soma	Vedic drink offered to gods; juice of Ephedra stalk; moon
Sompati Masya	New moon day that falls on a Monday that is especially sacred to ancestors
Stupa	Buddhist funeral mound containing relics of a teacher
Sukkah	Pleasure
Sumangali	Married woman whose husband is alive
Sushumna	Central channel of the body
Sutaka	The period of pollution following the death of a relative
Sva-dharma	One's own duty based on family vocation and stage of life
Svadha	The exclamation when offering food to the dead
Swadhyay	Self-study
Swarga	Paradise, full of pleasure
Swayambhu	Self-created
Tantra	Occult practices that value the body
Tanu	The body
Tapasya	The churning of spiritual fire
Tarpan	Offering water to ancestors
Theyyam	Spirit of the ancestor worshipped as a deity in North Kerala
Tirtha-shradh	Feeding the dead at a pilgrim place

Tripundra	Destroyer of three cities, a title of Shiva
Ucchaishrava	Flying celestial horse that is white and radiant
Ucchista	Leftover food
Vaikuntha	Abode of Vishnu, a higher heaven where everyone is fed
Vanaprastha ashrama	Stage of retirement when a person withdraws to a (metaphorical) forest
Varna-dharma	Following caste duty, or family vocation
Varshik-shradh	Death anniversary
Vetala	Ghost enslaved by sorcerer or a guardian-ghost
Vidhava	Widow
Viragal	Hero memorial stone
Visarjan	Immersion in water, bidding farewell
Vriddhi	Growth
Vriddhi-shradh	Feeding the ancestors at a family celebration, such as marriage
Yagna-shala	Vedic ritual ground
Yama-lok	The land of the dead ruled by Yama
Yogini	Occult priestesses, goddesses, experts
Yoni	Womb
Yuga	Era of the world; four eras make a lifespan of the world

Bibliography

Dongier, W., *Hindu Myths: A Sourcebook Translated from the Sanskrit.* New Delhi: Penguin Books, 1975.

——, *Origins of Evil in Hindu Mythology.* New Delhi: Motilal Banarsidass Publishing House, 1988.

——, *The Rig Veda: An Anthology.* New Delhi: Penguin Books, 1994.

Flood, Gavin, *An Introduction to Hinduism.* New Delhi: Cambridge University Press, 1998.

Gardiner, E., *Hindu Hell: Visions, Tours and Descriptions of the Infernal Otherworld,* second edition. New York: Italica Press, 2013.

Hart, George L. and Hank Heifetz (trs), *The Four Hundred Songs of War and Wisdom: An Anthology of Poems from Classical Tamil, the Purananuru,* New York: Columbia University Press, 2002.

Kinsley, David, *Hindu Goddesses: Visions of the Divine Feminine in the Hindu Religious Tradition.* Delhi: Motilal Banarsidass Publishing House, 1987.

Knipe K.M. (ed.), *The Hindu Rite of Entry into Heaven and Other Essays on Death and Ancestors in Hinduism.* Delhi: Motilal Banarsidass Publishing House, 2019.

Mani, Vettam, *Puranic Encyclopaedia: A Comprehensive Dictionary with Special Reference to the Epic and Puranic Literature.* Delhi: Motilal Banarsidass Publishing House, 1996.

Olivelle, P. and D.R. David, Jr (eds), *The Oxford History of Hinduism: Hindu Law*. New Delhi: Oxford University Press, 2018.

Pandey, R., *Hindu Samskaras: Socio-Religious Study of the Hindu Sacraments*. Delhi: Motilal Banarsidass Publishing House, 1969.

Saraswati, Swami Dayanand, translation by Vaidyanath Shastri. *The Sanskar Vidhi*. Sarvadeshik Arya Pratinidhi Sabha: New Delhi, 1985.

Sayers, M.R., *Feeding the Dead: Ancestor Worship in Ancient India*. New York: Oxford University Press, 2013.

Shastri, Dakshina Ranjan. *Origin and Development of the Rituals of Ancestor Worship in India*. Bookland Private: Calcutta, 1963.

Storm, Mary. *Head and Heart: Valour and Self-Sacrifice in the Art of India*. Routledge: New Delhi, 2013.

Walker, Benjamin. *Hindu World, An Encyclopedic Survey of Hinduism (2 volumes)*. New Delhi: Indus, 1968.

Walls, J.L. (ed.), *The Oxford Handbook of Eschatology*. New York: Oxford University Press, 2008.

Wilkins, W.J., *Hindu Mythology*. New Delhi: Rupa Publications, 1997.

Wood, E. and S.V. Subrahmanyam, *The Garuda Purana*. New York: AMS Press, 1974.

Zimmer, Heinrich, *Myths and Symbols in Indian Art and Civilization*. Delhi: Motilal Banarsidass, 1990.

Acknowledgements

To Shri Devdutt Chhatre, Vedic ritual specialist from Pune, who has helped clarify many doubts.

To Smt. Seema Sontakke, for researching and translating passages from the Samhitas and Brahmana literature.

Other titles by
Devdutt Pattanaik

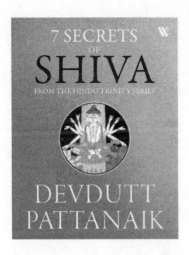

7 SECRETS OF SHIVA

In the living tradition that is Hinduism, divinity manifests as the Goddess, who embodies the world, as Shiva, who seeks to withdraw from the world, and as Vishnu, who engages with the world. This series explores their art, rituals, stories and relevance in modern times.

Smeared with ash
Draped in animal hide
He sits atop the snow-capped mountain
Skull in hand
Withdrawn, with dogs for company
Destroying the world with his indifference
He is God who the Goddess shall awaken
His name is Shiva

Locked in his stories, symbols and rituals are the secrets of our ancestors.

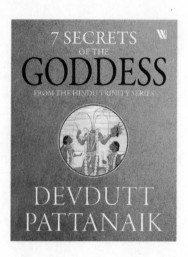

7 SECRETS OF THE GODDESS

In the living tradition that is Hinduism, divinity manifests as the Goddess, who embodies the world, as Shiva, who seeks to withdraw from the world, and as Vishnu, who engages with the world. This series explores their art, rituals, stories and relevance in modern times.

As nature, she is mother
As culture, she is daughter
Creator of humanity
Creation of humanity
She is wealth, power, language
Lakshmi, Durga, Saraswati
She is Devi
Answer to that masculine anxiety Which keeps resisting enquiry

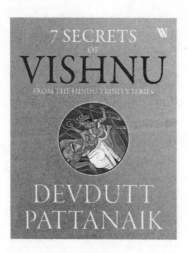

7 SECRETS OF VISHNU

In the living tradition that is Hinduism, divinity manifests as the Goddess, who embodies the world, as Shiva, who seeks to withdraw from the world, and as Vishnu, who engages with the world. This series explores their art, rituals, stories and relevance in modern times.

Anointed with perfumes
Draped in silk
He reclines on the ocean of milk
Eyes open
Ever smiling
Securing the world with his attention
He is God who is chased by fortune
Perumal, Balaji, Narayana, Vishnu
Who walks the earth as Krishna, and as Ram

7 SECRETS FROM
HINDU CALENDAR ART

Hindu mythology abounds with fascinating gods, goddesses and characters whose visual representations—through calendar art—are equally colourful. Hindu calendar art may seem fantastic and kitsch, but it is in fact the most democratic expression of a mythic imagery that was once restricted to temple walls and palm leaf manuscripts. These portraits of the Hindu pantheon of gods and the stories that surround them can be found on the walls and puja rooms of almost every Hindu household in India. Rich in symbols, each image is a piece of an ancient metaphysical jigsaw puzzle. In this book, Dr Devdutt Pattanaik, India's renowned mythologist, decodes these symbols to reveal a wisdom that has nourished India for thousands of years.